THE RESCUE FANTASY

SM Dyer

The Rescue Fantasy: Why Capable Women Stay Stuck and How to Reclaim the Power to Lead Your Life

Published by Aligned Living Press

This book is a work of nonfiction. The real stories included are based on composite experiences and have been modified to protect individual privacy. Any resemblance to specific individuals is coincidental.

First published 2026

Contents

— —

1	The Rescue Fantasy	1
2	You Already Have What You Need	13
3	Counting What Counts	25
4	The Permission Loop	37
5	Your Internal Scorecard	49
6	Setting Boundaries Without Guilt	61
7	Building Daily Self-Leadership Habits	73
8	When Old Patterns Return	83
9	Money and Self-Leadership	97
10	Your Support System	113
11	Creating Meaning Without External Milestones	125
12	The Practice of Self-Celebration	137
13	Leading Through Uncertainty	149
14	Your Ongoing Practice	163

About the Author 174

A Note from the Author

I wrote this book for the woman who is capable of far more than her current circumstances reflect. You know who you are.

You are not here because you lack ability. You are not here because the timing is wrong or the conditions aren't right or because you haven't found the right person to open the right door. You are here because you have been waiting, and the waiting has become so familiar it no longer feels like a choice.

This book is about that pattern. Where it comes from, how it works, and how to interrupt it. Not with motivation or affirmation, but with clarity, the kind that comes from seeing your own story plainly and deciding to write a different one.

You already have everything you need. This book is simply the moment the waiting ends and the work—the real, deliberate, self-directed work, begins.

SM Dyer

CHAPTER 1

The Rescue Fantasy

How the Waiting Pattern Quietly Shapes Capable Women's Lives

— —

Before we can move forward, we need to understand where we've been, and why.

This chapter isn't about judgment. It's about recognition. It's about looking at the story you've been living with compassion, curiosity, and honesty.

The Rescue Fantasy is not about romance. It's about postponement. It's the belief that life improves when something outside of your control changes. It's the belief that your life begins after something external changes.

After the degree. After the move. After the promotion. After the certification. After the timing feels right.

The truth is simpler, and more demanding: your life begins the moment you decide to lead it.

You're here because some part of you knows it's time for something different. Not because you've been doing everything wrong, but because you're ready to do things differently.

The Story We've All Been Told

We've all grown up with the same narrative, told in slightly different ways: wait. Be patient. Be good enough, educated enough, accomplished enough, prepared enough, and eventually your real life will begin.

Opportunity will notice you. Circumstances will align. Something or someone will arrive and unlock the life you've been waiting to live.

This story shows up everywhere. In fairy tales where a woman waits in a tower for rescue to arrive. In movies where the protagonist's real life begins after a turning-point event outside her control. In songs about being incomplete without something external. In well-meaning advice about waiting for the 'right time' or the 'right partner.' In social media that celebrates external milestones as the ultimate markers of a life going well.

The story is so pervasive that it becomes invisible. It stops sounding like a story and starts sounding like reality. You don't notice you're waiting because waiting has been reframed as wisdom: as patience, as prudence, as not getting ahead of yourself. The woman who launches before she feels ready is reckless. The woman who waits until conditions are right is sensible. Except the conditions never fully arrive, and sensible turns out to be another word for stuck.

What makes this particular form of waiting so durable is that it is not passive. It is active in all the ways that feel productive: researching, preparing, accumulating, planning. You are doing things. You simply are not doing the one thing that would change anything, committing to a direction and moving. The busyness of preparation becomes a sophisticated substitute for the vulnerability of action.

The Rescue Fantasy infiltrates every corner of life. We wait for the right job instead of creating our own opportunities. We wait for our circumstances to change before we start living fully. We wait for the perfect home in the perfect neighborhood before decorating. We wait for another qualification before speaking with authority. We wait for more confidence before taking responsibility. We wait for the 'right partner' before fully building the life we want.

The Rescue Fantasy isn't about romance. It's about agency, or the lack of it. It's the belief that your life is something that happens to you rather than something you create.

REAL STORY

Sarah, 34, had always wanted to travel to Italy. But she kept telling herself she'd go 'when she met someone to go with.' Years passed. Relationships came and went. The trip never happened.

One day she realized: she wasn't waiting for a travel companion. She was waiting for permission to want something just for herself. Three months later, she booked a solo trip. It changed everything—not because Italy was magical, but because she finally stopped waiting.

The Rescue Fantasy is seductive because it protects us. If we're waiting for something else to start our lives, we can't fail. We can't be disappointed. We can't be held accountable for missed opportunities. But protection comes at a cost.

Where This Story Came From, And Why It's Not Your Fault

Let's be very clear: the Rescue Fantasy isn't something you invented. Waiting once made sense. Dependence was survival. The world changed; the pattern didn't.

For generations, particularly for women, dependence wasn't romantic. It was survival. Economic systems limited independence. Legal frameworks denied rights. Social structures punished deviation. Generations of people didn't have choices we take for granted. They couldn't own property. Couldn't have bank accounts. Couldn't work certain jobs. Couldn't leave marriages easily. Couldn't vote.

In that context, waiting made sense. It was adaptation to reality. But the structures changed. The story didn't.

We now have access to education, careers, financial independence, and legal rights that previous generations fought for. Yet many of us still carry the belief that our real lives begin after something external unlocks them.

Cultural narratives travel in the body before they reach the mind. The message that a woman's life is oriented toward something arriving, toward completion by way of external circumstances, does not announce itself as a limitation. It arrives as a feeling: the sense that what you have now is preliminary, that the real version of your life is still ahead, contingent on something not yet in place. That feeling is so familiar it can be mistaken for reality. It can be mistaken for an accurate read of your situation rather than a story you inherited.

This matters because you cannot challenge a story you cannot see. The work of this book begins, necessarily, with naming it—not to assign blame for having absorbed it, but to create the small but essential gap between you and it. You are not the story. You absorbed the story. Those are different things, and the difference is where your agency lives.

Cultural narratives have incredible staying power. The work isn't blaming yourself for absorbing them, it's consciously choosing to release them. Waiting made sense. But it no longer serves you.

Understanding Your 'Why' Without Judgment

The Rescue Fantasy persists because it serves purposes. When we understand those purposes, we can find healthier ways to meet the same needs.

1. **Protection from Risk and Failure:** When you're waiting for permission or opportunities, you're protected from the vulnerability of putting yourself fully into your life. If things don't work out, you can point to circumstances, timing, location, or lack of support. The fantasy keeps you safe from the discomfort of full accountability.

2. **Safety from Social Judgment:** There's less social pressure when you're 'waiting for the right opportunity' than when you're actively choosing a different path. Waiting is culturally acceptable, even sympathized with. Boldly building a life you love independently can invite questions, concern, or unsolicited advice about what you 'should' be doing.

3. **Avoidance of Discomfort:** If you're waiting for connection to arrive, you don't have to fully feel what it's like to be alone right now. You can live in an imagined future where rescue comes, rather than sitting with the present moment as it is. The fantasy keeps difficult emotions at arm's length by promising they're temporary.

4. **Postponement of Hard Decisions:** When you're waiting for something or someone else to shape your future or validate your ideas, you don't have to make definitive choices about where to live, what career to pursue, or how to spend your resources. The fantasy allows you to keep all options open indefinitely, avoiding the discomfort of commitment and the grief of closing doors.

5. **Hope Without Effort:** The fantasy lets you feel hopeful about the future without requiring present action. You can believe your life will improve without having to do the difficult work of improving it. It's passive optimism, comforting in the short term, quietly corrosive over time.

Read that list not as a catalog of failings but as a portrait of a mind doing its job. Each of these functions is a rational response to real conditions—the genuine risk of failure, the real social cost of deviation, the actual discomfort of uncertainty. The Rescue Fantasy is not evidence of weakness. It is evidence of a mind working hard to protect you from pain.

The question is not whether the protection was reasonable. In many cases it was. The question is whether it is still serving you, or whether the cost of the protection has begun to exceed the cost of the thing it is protecting you from. For most women reading this book, the answer is yes. The waiting is now costing more than the risk of moving would.

The real question is not: 'Am I weak for wanting these protections?' The real question is: 'What do I need to feel ready to lead?' And the honest answer, most of the time, is: less than you think.

The Hidden Cost of the Waiting Room

While you're waiting, life is happening. Days turn into months, months into years. And at some point, you look up and realize you've been so focused on waiting for your life to begin that you forgot to live it.

1. **Lost Time and Opportunities:** You postpone travel, career moves, investments, experiences, dreams, telling yourself you'll do them 'when.' When you meet someone. When the kids are grown. When you relocate. When circumstances align. When you feel ready. But that 'when' keeps receding into the future. The opportunities don't wait for you to be ready. Time doesn't pause.
2. **Diminished Self-Trust:** Each time you wait, you teach yourself that you are not capable of moving forward without

external conditions changing first. Over time, that story hardens. What began as a temporary pause becomes a fixed belief about who you are and what you can do.

3. **Unmet Potential:** There are versions of yourself you'll never meet if you keep waiting. The one who takes bold risks. Who builds something meaningful. Who discovers what she's truly capable of when she stops holding back. That person exists, but only if you stop waiting and start moving.
4. **Accumulated Resentment:** Waiting breeds bitterness. At first, it's subtle, frustration with people who seem to have what you want. Over time it deepens into resentment toward yourself for not choosing differently, toward others for not rescuing you, toward life itself for not unfolding the way you expected.
5. **The Weight of Regret:** Perhaps the heaviest cost: looking back and realizing you gave years to a story that was never true. That you were always capable of more than you believed. That the only person who could save you was you—and you were right there all along, waiting for permission you never needed.

These costs are worth sitting with, because the Rescue Fantasy obscures them almost by design. One of the things waiting does most efficiently is prevent you from feeling how much it is costing you. The vague sense of life-on-hold is more diffuse, more manageable, less acute than the sharp discomfort of moving toward something uncertain. The waiting feels like safety. The costs accrue quietly, off to the side, until the day you do the accounting and find the total is higher than you imagined.

Recognizing these costs is not about generating regret for time already spent. It is about making a different calculation going forward, one that weighs the real cost of continued waiting against the real cost of beginning to move, with everything you currently have, toward the life you have been postponing.

Moving Forward with Grace

This chapter has asked you to look honestly at patterns that may have been operating for years, maybe decades. That takes courage.

If you're feeling uncomfortable right now, if you're recognizing yourself in these pages in ways that sting a little, that's okay. That's actually good. It means you're paying attention. It means you're ready.

But here's what's crucial: awareness without action is just another version of waiting. You can recognize patterns and still tell yourself you'll change 'when you're ready' or 'when it feels easier' or 'when you're more prepared.' That's just the Rescue Fantasy in a different costume: waiting for future-you to save present-you.

The alternative is grace. Grace means recognizing that you did the best you could with the awareness you had at the time, and then choosing differently going forward. Not someday. Not when it's comfortable. Now.

Before moving to the next chapter, it is worth pausing with two questions, not to write answers on a page, but to let them work on you. The first: where in your life are you still waiting for permission to begin? Not in the abstract, but specifically, the actual area, the actual thing you have been telling yourself requires some prior condition to be met. And then: who do you believe must grant that permission? Name them, if you can. Because the moment you can name the person whose approval you are waiting for, you can also ask the obvious follow-up: are they actually coming? And if not, what are you really waiting for?

The second question is sharper: what have you postponed because you believed the timing wasn't right? Not the vague sense that things haven't lined up, but the specific thing—the project, the conversation, the move, the beginning. And what is the condition you're waiting to improve? Write it down if you need to. Then look at it directly and ask: is that condition necessary for a first step? Or is it a story about what's necessary, one that sounds like prudence but functions like postponement?

ACTION STEPS

Before moving to the next chapter, take these three actions:

1. **Identify one specific way you have been waiting in your life.** Not all of them, just one. The clearest one. Write it down somewhere you will see it. This is your starting point, not your final destination.
2. **Acknowledge the reason the waiting once made sense.** Say out loud, yes, actually speak the words, 'I have been

waiting for [specific thing], and that made sense given [your reason]. I'm ready to choose differently now.' Notice what it feels like to say it without judgment. The act of speaking it is itself a small act of self-leadership.

3. **Take one small action within the next 24 hours.** Identify one small action you have been postponing that you could take in the next twenty-four hours. Not a life-changing decision. Something simple that honors your agency. Make the call. Send the email. Do the thing. Practice not waiting.

The point of these actions is not their scale. It is the pattern they establish. Every time you act without waiting for permission, you build evidence, against the story that you cannot, and for the story that you can. That evidence accumulates. It becomes the foundation of the work ahead.

You were never waiting for rescue. You were waiting for a decision. And that decision, that single, unspectacular, completely available decision to take the next step, is the one that changes everything.

In the next chapter, we'll examine the many guises the Rescue Fantasy can take, so you can recognize it the moment it appears.

CHAPTER 2

You Already Have What You Need

Recognizing the Power and Capability You Already Possess

— —

You already have enough to begin. You just need to believe that.

In Chapter 1, we examined the belief that life begins after something external changes. Now we confront something more uncomfortable: the realization that you've had more power than you've been exercising all along.

This isn't about pretending you have resources you don't. It's about acknowledging resources you do have but have been discounting, postponing, or waiting for permission to use.

The shift required here is internal, not external. From: 'I need more before I can begin.' To: 'I have enough to take the next right step.'

The Credential Trap

One of the most insidious forms of the Rescue Fantasy is what we'll call the Credential Trap. It works like this: you want to start something, a business, a new career direction, a creative project, a leadership role. But you tell yourself you can't. Not yet. Not until you get another degree or certification, complete one more course, wait for someone with power to validate your readiness, accumulate more years of experience, or feel confident enough, someday.

Here's the problem: credentials don't install agency. They can open doors. They can signal competence. They can provide valuable knowledge. But they cannot give you permission to lead your own life. Only you can do that.

The Credential Trap keeps you perpetually preparing and never acting. It's waiting, dressed up as responsibility. Preparation can become procrastination with better branding.

The belief that you need one more credential before you can begin is often a fear of full accountability disguised as prudence. It's not that you're not ready, it's that being ready means you can no longer blame lack of preparation if things don't work out.

REAL STORY

Paula, 38, wanted to transition from corporate finance to freelance consulting. But she kept telling herself she needed an MBA first. 'How can I advise companies without the credential?' she reasoned.

> After three years of waiting for the 'right time' to start the MBA program, a former colleague asked if she'd consult on a project. Paula almost said no, she didn't have the MBA yet. Then she paused. She had fifteen years of finance experience. She had solved exactly the problem this client faced. The MBA wouldn't teach her what she already knew. She said yes. The project went well. Then another came. Then another. Two years later, Paula realized: the MBA was never about learning. It was about permission she never really needed.

The degree was never the gatekeeper. The decision was. Credentials aren't worthless — they're just not the gatekeepers we make them out to be. The question isn't: 'Am I qualified?' The question is: 'Do I have what's needed to take the next right step?' Usually, the answer is yes, and what's needed is action.

There is a particular cruelty in the Credential Trap, which is that it looks most convincing to the most capable people. The woman with fifteen years of genuine expertise can generate a more compelling case for needing one more qualification than the woman with two years of experience ever could, because she has enough knowledge to see exactly where her gaps are, and a sophisticated enough mind to construct an argument for why those gaps are disqualifying. Her intelligence, in other words, is being deployed against her.

The way out is to ask a different question. Not 'am I fully qualified?', which may never produce a confident yes, but 'do I know enough to be useful to someone right now?' That question is answerable. And the answer, for most capable women in the Credential Trap, is yes. Useful enough to begin, and to build from there.

The Myth of Readiness

There's a belief that underlies much of our waiting: the belief that readiness is a feeling that arrives before action. That one day you'll wake up feeling confident, prepared, certain, and then you'll act. This is backwards. Readiness doesn't precede action. Readiness emerges through action. You don't feel ready and then start. You start, and through starting, you become ready.

No parent feels fully ready before their first child arrives. No entrepreneur feels prepared before launching. No leader feels confident before their first major decision. No artist feels certain before creating their first significant work. They act anyway. And through acting, they develop the capabilities that confidence is built from.

Waiting for readiness is waiting for certainty. Certainty arrives after movement.

Confidence isn't what you need before you act. It's what you build by acting despite uncertainty. Every person you admire as confident got there by doing things while not feeling ready.

What this means for your specific version of waiting is this: there is no version of more preparation that will produce the feeling you are waiting for. That feeling is produced by starting. By the first conversation that goes awkwardly and then well. By the first decision made without certainty and then survived. By the first thing attempted without full credentials and then, to your moderate surprise, done adequately. The evidence of your readiness is not available in advance. It is available only on the other side of beginning, and the only way to access it is to begin.

Power You Already Have

Let's look clearly at the power you possess right now. Not the power you wish you had. Not the power you think you need. The power you have today.

1. **Experience:** This is the first form of power, and it is the one most consistently undervalued. You have lived a life that has taught you things. Challenges navigated, mistakes absorbed, situations handled that were not in any syllabus. This is knowledge, genuine, embodied, earned knowledge, even when no institution has credentialed it. The woman who has managed a difficult relationship, led a team through a crisis, built something from nothing, raised a child, or simply kept going through circumstances that were genuinely hard has developed competence that cannot be replicated in a classroom. That competence is power, whether you are counting it or not.

2. **Pattern Recognition:** The capacity to read a situation, sense when something is off before you can fully articulate why, identify an opportunity before it has been validated by consensus. This intuition or 'gut feeling' is not mystical. It is the product of accumulated experience; a kind of fast processing built from everything you have observed and survived. It is also the kind of intelligence most easily dismissed by the woman who possesses it: 'I'm not sure why,

I just have a feeling.' That feeling is data. It deserves to be treated as such.

3. **Choice:** The power that is always available and almost always underestimated. You can say yes. You can say no. You can redirect your time, your energy, your attention. You can commit to something and mean it, or decline something and hold that boundary. This sounds simple until you notice how rarely it is exercised fully—how often the choices that matter most are deferred, hedged, or framed as not really choices at all. They are choices. You are making them whether you acknowledge that or not.

4. **Self-definition:** The power to decide what your life is about. Not what other people expect it to be about, not what the cultural script prescribes, but what you are genuinely building toward, what you are willing to sacrifice for, what you refuse to trade away. This power is available to you regardless of your circumstances. It does not require permission, resources, or the right conditions. It requires only the willingness to ask the question and to sit with an honest answer.

5. **Present Action:** The power to move today, right now, without waiting for conditions to improve. This is the power the rescue fantasy most directly suppresses, and it is also the most fundamental: the recognition that you can act now. Not perfectly, not with full preparation, not with a guarantee of the outcome. But now. That is always available. The question is whether you are willing to use it.

How much of that power have you been holding in reserve? Waiting to deploy until you felt 'ready enough' or 'qualified enough' or 'worthy enough'? The waiting hasn't been about lack of power. It's been about underestimating the power you already have.

> **REAL STORY**
>
> Priya, 31, wanted to write about mental health. But she kept thinking she needed a psychology degree first. 'Who am I to write about this?' she'd ask herself. Then she remembered: she'd lived with anxiety for over ten years. She'd tried several different therapists. She'd read dozens of books on the subject. She'd developed coping strategies through trial and error. She'd helped friends navigate their own struggles. She didn't need a degree to share her experience. She had power through living it.
>
> She started writing. Within weeks, her articles were being shared thousands of times online. Not because she had credentials, because she had insight earned through experience.

The Permission Paradox

Here's a strange truth: the people who are most qualified to do something are often the ones who wait longest for permission. Why? Because they understand the complexity of what they're attempting. They see how much they don't know. They're aware of their limitations. Meanwhile, people with less knowledge charge ahead confidently, because they don't know what they don't know.

Competence → Awareness of limitations → Delay → Wait for permission or qualification → Delay

This is the Permission Paradox: awareness of your limitations can become the thing that stops you from using your strengths. You focus on what you lack and discount what you have. The solution isn't to become delusionally confident. It's to accurately assess what you do know, what you can do, and what next step is appropriate given that reality. You don't need to be an expert to begin. You need to know enough to be useful to the person one step behind you.

Leading your own life doesn't mean you have all the answers. It means you're willing to take the next step even when you don't. Personal power isn't about certainty, it's about agency.

The Permission Paradox has a particular shape in the lives of capable women. Competence, it turns out, produces its own kind of waiting, not the waiting of someone who doesn't know enough, but the waiting of someone who knows too much about the gap between where she is and where she thinks she needs to be before she can legitimately proceed. The more you understand about a domain, the more visible its complexity becomes, and the more that complexity can be used to justify continued preparation rather than current action.

The way through is not to pretend the complexity doesn't exist. It is to ask a different question: not 'am I ready for the full scope of this?' but 'am I ready for the next step?' Those are almost never the same question, and conflating them is how capable women stay stuck. You do not need to be ready for the whole thing. You need to be ready for what is immediately in front of you—which, in most cases, you already are.

The Location Illusion, When Geography Becomes Rescue

A specific version of the Rescue Fantasy deserves attention: the Location Illusion. This is the belief that if you could just move—to a different city, a different country, a different continent, everything would change. And it's true that location can matter. Access to opportunities varies by geography. Cultural context shapes possibility. Legal frameworks differ.

But here's what doesn't change with location: your relationship to your own agency. If you're waiting for permission now, you'll wait for permission there. If you're discounting your power now, you'll discount it there. If you're postponing decisions now, you'll postpone them there. Location can expand opportunity. But it cannot install self-leadership. Geography changes context. It does not change identity.

> **REAL STORY**
>
> Mary, 29, was convinced she needed to move from Nigeria to the UK to 'really succeed.' She spent three years focused entirely on immigration paperwork, putting everything else on hold. 'Once I get there,' she'd say, 'then I'll start my business.'
>
> Finally, a mentor asked her a hard question: 'What would you do if you knew you were staying here permanently?' Mary realized she'd been using the immigration dream as a reason not to act where she was. She started the business in Lagos. Within a year, it was profitable. She still wanted to travel and potentially relocate, but now from a position of strength, not rescue.

This doesn't mean you shouldn't move. It means geography shouldn't be where you store your agency. Lead your life now, where you are, with what you have. Then, if you choose to move, you're moving to expand, not to escape.

The Location Illusion is worth examining carefully because it is one of the more convincing forms of the rescue fantasy. Unlike waiting for a partner or a credential, waiting for the right geography can marshal genuine evidence: opportunities really are distributed unevenly, certain industries really do cluster in particular cities, some legal and social environments really are more enabling than others. All of that is true. None of it changes the underlying question.

The question is not whether a different location would offer more. Almost certainly it would, in some ways and for some things. The question is whether the agency you are not currently exercising would suddenly be available to you in a different place—and the honest answer is that it would not, because the constraint is not geographical. The woman who is waiting in Lagos for London to unlock her potential will, with high probability, find a new reason to wait once she arrives in London. Not because London isn't better in some respects, but because the pattern of waiting travels with her. It always does. The work is to interrupt the pattern where you are.

From 'Not Enough' to 'Next Step'

The shift this chapter asks you to make is simple in concept, difficult in practice: stop asking 'do I have enough?' and start asking 'what can I do with what I have?' This is the shift from scarcity thinking to agency thinking.

Scarcity thinking → focus on missing resources → delay

Agency thinking → focus on available resources → action

Scarcity thinking focuses on what's missing: I don't have the degree, the connections, the experience, the confidence, the resources. Agency thinking focuses on what's present: I have experience from my current role, one person who believes in me, access to free online resources, evenings and weekends, the ability to start small.

Both assessments might be factually accurate. But they lead to radically different actions. Scarcity thinking postpones. Agency thinking acts. You don't need to have everything figured out. You just need to know the next right step.

This reframe is deceptively simple and worth spending time with. The question 'do I have enough?' has no satisfying answer, because 'enough' has no fixed definition. It expands to accommodate whatever you currently have, always pointing to what is just beyond it. It is a question designed, structurally, to produce the answer 'not quite yet.' The question 'what can I do with what I have?' is different in kind: it is answerable, it is actionable, and it directs attention toward movement rather than assessment.

The shift from one to the other is not a matter of optimism or positive thinking. It is a matter of which question you choose to hold as the primary one. Both are available to you at any moment. One keeps you in the waiting room. The other gets you moving.

ACTION STEPS

Before moving to the next chapter, take these three actions.

1. **Identify one area where you have been waiting for credentials.** What have you been postponing until you have 'one more' degree, certification, or qualification? Then ask: what do I already know that would allow me to take one small step right now?
2. **For each of the five power types explored in this chapter:** experience, pattern recognition, choice, self-definition, and present action, identify one specific, concrete instance in your own life where that power has been present. Not a general acknowledgment that you probably have it somewhere, but a real example: an actual thing you did, a moment when that capacity showed up, a choice you made or could have made. Acknowledge them. Evidence matters more than feelings here, and you have more evidence than you are currently counting.
3. **Identify your next right step.** Not your ultimate goal. Not the perfect plan. Just the next right step you can take with the power you have right now. Then take it. This week. Don't wait for permission that isn't coming.

You're not waiting to become someone qualified to lead your life. You do not become qualified to lead your life. You decide to. The qualification was never the issue. The decision is the whole thing, and it has been waiting for you the entire time.

CHAPTER 3

Counting What Counts

Taking Honest Inventory of the Assets You Already Possess

— —

In the previous chapters, we've examined the Rescue Fantasy and recognized that you have more power than you've been exercising.

You cannot use what you refuse to count.

Now it's time to get specific. To look at your life as it is, not as it 'should' be, not as you wish it were, but as it is; and take honest inventory.

This isn't about gratitude as obligation. It's not about pretending challenges don't exist. It's about accurate assessment. Because you can't lead your life effectively if you're operating from a distorted view of what you're working with. Inventory corrects distortion.

The Problem with Deficit Thinking

Most of us have been trained in deficit thinking, the habit of focusing on what's missing rather than what's present. We scan our lives for gaps: not enough money, not enough time, not enough experience, not enough connections, not enough confidence.

Deficit thinking feels responsible. It often becomes habitual minimization. This isn't wrong, constraints are real. But when deficit thinking becomes your default lens, you miss what's available to you. You overlook resources. You discount skills. You minimize accomplishments. Minimization is not humility. It is habitual miscalculation. You fail to leverage what you have because you're so focused on what you lack.

Inventory isn't about denying problems. It's about seeing the whole picture, including the assets you've been taking for granted. Inventory is not optimism. It is precision. It is the discipline of seeing what is present.

Deficit thinking has a particular relationship with competence that is worth naming. The more capable you are, the more accurately you can identify what you're missing, and the more persuasively you can argue for why those gaps are disqualifying. Incompetent people cannot construct a compelling case for their own inadequacy. Capable people can, and they do, with impressive regularity.

This is not a failure of self-awareness. It is, in a perverse way, a misapplication of analytical skill: the same rigor that makes you good at your work gets turned inward and used to build an inventory of everything you lack rather than everything you have. The result is an assessment that is technically accurate, yes, those gaps are real, but structurally incomplete, because it systematically excludes the other side of the ledger.

Taking honest inventory means doing the full accounting, not just the half that confirms the waiting. It means looking at what is present with the same precision you bring to what is absent. Not to manufacture false confidence, but to correct a genuine distortion—because you cannot make good decisions from a picture that is missing half the information.

What Inventory Actually Means

Taking inventory means documenting what you have—skills, relationships, resources, knowledge. It means acknowledging what you've accomplished, even if it feels small. It means recognizing patterns of strength: what you do well consistently. And it means identifying untapped assets, what you have but aren't currently using.

This creates a foundation for action. You can't build strategy without knowing what materials you're working with. What you refuse to count, you cannot leverage.

The word 'inventory' has a deliberate precision. An inventory is not a mood assessment or a 'feelings check'. It is a count: specific, documented, and resistant to the distortions that memory and confidence levels produce when left unexamined. When a business takes inventory, it counts what is on the shelves, not what might be or what there was last quarter. The same discipline applies here.

Most people have a rough, impressionistic sense of their own skills and resources, a general feeling of 'I'm reasonably capable in this area' or 'I have some connections.' The problem with impressionistic assessment is that it is vulnerable to mood. On a confident day, your capabilities look substantial. On a difficult day, the same capabilities seem inadequate. An actual inventory, specific, written, evidenced, is not vulnerable to mood in the same way. It is a document, not a feeling, and it can be consulted on the difficult days when feelings are not reliable guides to what is true.

Taking Stock: Skills and Capabilities

When most people try to list their skills, they begin and end with the professional ones, the capabilities that appear on a CV, that have been named in a performance review, that carry formal recognition. These are worth documenting. But they represent only a fraction of what you know how to do, and often not the most relevant fraction.

Consider the full range of what you are genuinely capable of. The professional skills: what you have been trained in, what you have developed through repeated application, what people seek you out for within your field. But also the life skills that rarely get counted as such: the capacity to manage a complex household, to navigate difficult interpersonal dynamics, to organize disparate resources toward a goal, to sustain effort through tedious or unglamorous work. These are not soft or secondary competencies. They are transferable capabilities, and many of them are genuinely rare.

Consider your creative capacities, not only the ones with obvious outlets, but the forms of creative thinking you apply to problems that are not labeled 'creative.' The ability to see connections others miss, to reframe a situation, to generate options where others see only constraints. And your interpersonal skills: the capacity to build trust, to read a room, to navigate conflict without destruction, to hold space for someone else's difficulty while maintaining your own steadiness. These things are competencies. They took years to build. They are worth counting.

Finally: what do you have that you almost never use? Skills acquired and then set aside. Knowledge accumulated in a context that no longer exists. Capabilities dormant from lack of occasion. These are assets, and they are yours, regardless of whether anyone is currently asking for them.

Write this inventory down, not in a template, but in whatever form makes it real for you. The goal is a document you can return to when you need a clear-eyed account of what you are really working with.

Taking Stock: Relationships and Support

The relationship inventory is easy to underdo, for a reason that is worth naming: we tend to count only the people we feel close to, and discount or overlook the wider network of people who have been, or could be, genuinely useful to us. A relationship inventory that only captures your closest friendships is as incomplete as a skills inventory that only captures your formal qualifications.

Think instead about the functions that a good support network serves. Who in your life provides genuine emotional support, not the people who listen patiently and then redirect to their own concerns, but the people who can hold your reality without trying to fix it or dismiss it? Who provides practical help when it is genuinely needed, without attaching conditions or keeping score? Who has relevant expertise or experience in areas where you are growing, and is accessible enough to be a real resource rather than a theoretical one?

The two functions most commonly absent from the support systems of capable, self-reliant women are accountability and honest feedback. Accountability, someone who holds you to your own stated intentions without rescuing you from the discomfort of following through, is rare because it requires a relationship strong enough to carry the occasional friction of being told 'you said you would do this, and you haven't.' Honest feedback is rare for the same reason: it requires both a relationship that can withstand the truth and a person willing to offer it regardless of whether it is welcome.

Map what you genuinely have across these areas. Note the gaps. And note something else: the people who are nominally providing support but are, in practice, maintaining your dependence rather than building your capacity. Those are not the same thing, and it is worth being clear about the difference.

Taking Stock: Accomplishments

The accomplishment audit is, for most women, the hardest part of this inventory, not because there is little to count, but because the discount mechanism is most active here. Achievements get reclassified: the thing that was hard becomes 'what anyone would have done,' the project that succeeded becomes 'I got lucky,' the transition navigated becomes 'I didn't have a choice.' The audit requires you to set the discount mechanism aside and count what actually happened.

Start with the last five years. What did you accomplish? Not only the things with external recognition attached, like the promotions, the degrees, the publicly visible wins; but the things that required sustained effort and produced a real outcome. Projects completed. Difficult situations navigated to a resolution. Things built that did not exist before you built them. Challenges encountered and survived, including the ones that did not produce a victory so much as a continuation, because continuing, in some circumstances, is itself a significant achievement.

Then go wider: what have you transitioned through? Transitions are among the most demanding things a person can do, and among the least counted, because they often feel like disruption rather than accomplishment. Moving. Changing careers. Ending a relationship. Starting over in some significant way. These required you to orient in unfamiliar territory, build competence under pressure, and keep going without the stability of established routine. That is capability. It counts.

Write the list. Make it specific. The goal is not to feel good about yourself, though that may happen. The goal is accuracy—a true account of what you have done, from which you can build an accurate sense of what you are capable of doing.

Recognizing Patterns of Strength

Look across the inventory you've just completed. What patterns emerge? What do you do consistently well? What do people ask you for help with? What challenges have you overcome more than once? What comes naturally that might be difficult for others?

Patterns matter more than individual instances, because patterns reveal something about who you consistently are rather than what you happened to do once. A single accomplishment might be attributed to luck or circumstances. A pattern cannot be. If you have navigated three difficult leadership situations well, that is not luck. If you have rebuilt after two significant setbacks, that is not circumstance. That is a demonstrated capacity: something you reliably have access to.

Look for the thread that runs across different domains: the skill that shows up whether you're at work, in a relationship, managing something personal, or in a new and unfamiliar situation. The quality that people who have known you in different contexts have all remarked on. The thing that feels natural to you but that you have watched others struggle with. That thread is your baseline competence—the thing you can count on, and from which almost everything else can be built.

Identify three to five of these patterns, and for each one, find the evidence: the specific instances that confirm it's a pattern and not an exception. That evidence is the foundation of your strategic self-assessment. It is not self-promotion. It is accuracy, and, in this context, accuracy is the most useful thing you can bring to the work ahead.

The Resource Gap vs. the Action Gap

After taking inventory, you'll likely notice two things: you have more than you thought, and some genuine gaps exist. The question becomes: which gaps are resource gaps, where you genuinely lack something necessary, and which are action gaps, where you have what you need but aren't using it?

Resource Gap → Acquisition required

Action Gap → Activation required

Resource gaps require acquisition. Action gaps require activation. We often mislabel action gaps as resource gaps because action requires exposure.

> **REAL STORY**
>
> Jennifer wanted to start freelancing but told herself she needed 'a proper website' first. That was a resource gap. Or was it? She had a laptop, internet access, basic design skills, and writing ability. She could create a simple one-page site in an afternoon using free tools. The real gap wasn't resources, it was the discomfort of putting herself out there before everything felt 'professional enough.' That's an action gap.
>
> Eventually she built the simple site. Started freelancing. Updated the site as she went. Two years later, she hired a professional designer, from a position of profit, not paralysis.

The resource-gap vs action-gap distinction is one of the more practically useful frameworks in this book, and it is worth applying with some rigor rather than using it simply to reassure yourself that all your gaps are action gaps. Some gaps really are resource gaps. Genuinely lacking the language skills to work in a particular market is a resource gap. Not having the legal status to work in a particular country is a resource gap. Needing specific technical knowledge that takes time to acquire is a resource gap. These are real, and pretending otherwise is not self-leadership. It is wishful thinking.

The discipline is in the honest assessment: when you say you cannot move forward because you lack something, is that true? What specifically do you lack, and is that specific thing genuinely required for the next step, or is it required for a later step that you are using to avoid taking the first one? Most of the time, the next step requires considerably less than the eventual destination. The website Jennifer needed to start freelancing was not the website she eventually wanted to have. Starting from the simpler version was not a compromise. It was the appropriate action for where she actually was.

Run this analysis on the thing you have been most persistently postponing. Be specific about what you believe is missing. Then ask whether it is missing for the next step or for a later one. In most cases, you will find the next step is available to you. The action gap, once named, is considerably less comfortable than the resource gap, because the resource gap offers a waiting room with a clear condition for exit, and the action gap offers only the discomfort of moving without a guarantee. But it also offers something the resource gap cannot: the actual beginning of movement.

ACTION STEPS

Before moving forward, take these three actions.

1. **Complete your inventory in writing.** Do not rely on mental reflection. Clarity requires documentation. Set aside thirty minutes and write down your skills, relationships, accomplishments, and patterns of strength. Use the frameworks from this chapter as your guide, but write in your own words. The goal is a document you can return to, a written record of what you actually have to work with.
2. **Identify three underutilized assets.** Choose three things you already possess—skills, connections, or resources, that you are not currently using fully. For each one, write down one concrete way you could activate it this month. Not eventually. This month.
3. **Reframe one deficit-based statement.** Take one thought of the form 'I don't have enough X' and rewrite it as: 'I have Y, which allows me to begin with Z.' This is not optimism. It is accuracy, the discipline of seeing what is present alongside what is absent, and making decisions from the full picture rather than half of it.

The inventory you have taken in this chapter is the foundation of everything that follows. Not because it is complete, no inventory of a living person is ever complete, but because it replaces a distorted picture with a more accurate one. You have more to work with than you have been counting. Some genuine gaps exist. Both things are true. From that full picture, built on evidence rather than habit, you can begin to make decisions and take action in a way that would not have been possible from the half-picture you started with.

In the next chapter, we move from inventory to direction, from knowing what you have to deciding what you are going to do with it. The counting was preparation. Now comes the choosing.

CHAPTER 4

The Permission Loop

How Waiting for Validation Keeps Capable Women Stuck

— —

You've recognized the patterns of waiting. You've acknowledged your existing power. You've taken stock.

Now comes the hardest part: making decisions and taking action without waiting for external permission, validation, or certainty.

This is where theory becomes practice. Where awareness becomes change.

Let's be honest about why this part is harder than everything that came before. Recognition is private. Inventory is internal. But decision-making is exposed. When you make a choice, you're putting yourself on record. You're saying: This was my call. And with that comes the possibility of being wrong, of being questioned, of having to own whatever comes next.

For women who have spent years operating inside the Permission Loop, consciously or not, that exposure can feel genuinely threatening. Not because they lack capability, but because they've been taught, and often systematically, that asserting their own judgment without external endorsement is risky. That lesson was sometimes delivered directly. More often it arrived quietly, through years of watching how confident women were received, through feedback that was more comfortable when framed as collaboration than as conviction.

This chapter is about dismantling that conditioning, not by talking yourself out of fear, but by building such a solid record of your own decision-making that the fear loses its authority.

The Permission Loop

Many of us are stuck in what I call the Permission Loop:

You want to do something. You seek external validation,'Is this a good idea?' Any hesitation reads as 'not yet.' You wait for more certainty. You repeat the loop.

The loop keeps you safe. It also keeps you stuck.

Breaking the loop requires making decisions from self-trust rather than external approval.

Self-trust isn't something you develop by thinking about it. You develop it by making decisions, seeing what happens, adjusting, and making more decisions. It's a muscle that strengthens with use.

The Permission Loop is particularly seductive because it masquerades as diligence. You're not procrastinating, you're being thorough. You're not avoiding accountability, you're being collaborative. You're not waiting for rescue, you're gathering input. These are all plausible explanations that can go unquestioned for years.

Here is the tell: when you notice that gathering more input rarely produces more clarity, when you find yourself in the same place after five opinions as you were after none, you're not in a research process. You're in a deferral process. The information isn't the point. The permission is.

There's also a subtler version of the loop that's worth naming: internal permission-seeking. This is when you don't need someone else to validate your decision, you need a future version of yourself to feel certain first. You wait until it 'feels right.' Until you're 'ready.' Until the anxiety drops to a level that feels acceptable before you'll move. This version of the loop is just as effective at keeping you stationary as the external one. Certainty is not a prerequisite for action. It is, more often, a product of it.

Auditing Where You're Waiting for Permission

Before you can break the Permission Loop, you need to see it clearly. Most of us have specific domains, particular kinds of decisions, where we reliably default to seeking external validation. Identifying yours is the first step.

Ask yourself: What decision have I been avoiding? Whose permission, explicit or implicit, am I waiting for? What do I fear will happen if I decide without that permission? And critically:

what evidence do I already have that I'm capable of handling that outcome?

Often the answers to these questions reveal patterns that have been invisible because they're so consistent. You might discover that you reliably defer to a particular person, a parent, a mentor, a partner, even in areas where their expertise is no greater than yours. You might find that the decisions you avoid tend to cluster around a specific type of risk: financial decisions, career decisions, decisions that involve public visibility. You might notice that your permission-seeking intensifies when the stakes feel higher, which is exactly the moment when your own judgment matters most.

It's also worth examining the secondary cost of permission-seeking that often goes unacknowledged: the message it sends to yourself. Every time you defer a decision until someone else validates it, you are implicitly confirming the belief that your own judgment isn't sufficient. Repeated often enough, it becomes a conviction. The antidote is not an affirmation—it's a decision, made and owned.

A Framework for Making Autonomous Decisions

When you're used to seeking permission, making autonomous decisions can feel overwhelming—not because you lack the capability, but because you've been out of practice. The following framework gives you a reliable structure to work through any decision you've been postponing.

Step 1: Name the Decision Precisely

Vague decisions stay in limbo because they're impossible to make. 'Should I change careers?' cannot be decided. 'Should I enroll in the data science bootcamp starting in January?' can. Specificity is not a small thing here, it's what makes the decision real and therefore actionable.

Step 2: Separate What You Know from What You're Assuming

Write down what is factually true about this situation. Then, separately, write down what you're assuming. Most decision paralysis lives in the assumption column, catastrophic outcomes that feel like certainties but are only possibilities. Seeing them distinguished on the page changes their weight.

Step 3: Identify the Values at Stake

Which of your core values does this decision touch? When a decision feels hard, it's often because two values are in tension, security and freedom, for example, or belonging and independence. Naming the tension doesn't resolve it, but it reframes the decision from 'what's right?' to 'what do I choose to prioritize here?' That is a question you are fully qualified to answer.

Step 4: Consider Realistic Outcomes

Walk through the best case, the worst case, and the most likely case. For the worst case specifically, ask: could I handle this? Not 'would I want to?' but 'am I capable of surviving and adapting to this outcome?' The answer, for most decisions, is yes. Acknowledging that transforms worst-case thinking from a reason not to decide into useful scenario planning.

Step 5: Set a Decision Deadline

Open-ended decisions stay open. Choose a specific date by which you will have made your decision. Tell someone if it helps. Put it in your calendar. The deadline is not arbitrary, it's a commitment to yourself that you will not let this decision continue to live in the waiting room indefinitely.

Step 6: Make the Call

Choose. Even if you're not certain. Especially if you're not certain. There is almost no decision that is improved by more waiting once you've done the work of the previous five steps. At some point, more time is not producing more clarity; it's just deferring accountability. That's the moment to decide.

Step 7: Commit to Learning, Not Just Outcomes

Your measure of a good decision should not be whether it produced the outcome you wanted. It should be whether you made it with the information and values available to you at the time, and whether you extracted useful learning from what followed. By that measure, most decisions, including the ones that don't work out, are good decisions.

When You Make the 'Wrong' Decision

Here's what permission-seeking protects you from: the possibility of being 'wrong.'

If someone else tells you what to do and it doesn't work out, you can blame them. If you decide for yourself and it doesn't work out, you have to own it. This is uncomfortable. It's also essential.

Because here's the truth about 'wrong' decisions: most of them aren't permanently wrong, they're data points. Wrong decisions teach you what right decisions look like. And making a decision and adjusting is almost always better than making no decision at all.

Decision → Outcome → Learning → Adjustment → Next Decision

> **REAL STORY**
>
> Anthea decided to leave her corporate job to start a consulting business. Six months in, she was struggling. Not enough clients. Burning through savings. By some measures, it was the 'wrong' decision. But through the struggle, she learned what she really wanted wasn't consulting, it was building products. She pivoted to a startup idea that had emerged from her consulting work. Three years later, that startup was acquired, making her incredibly financially successful 'overnight'.

Was leaving corporate the 'wrong' decision? Or was it the necessary step toward finding the right path? The goal isn't to make perfect decisions. It's to make decisions, learn from them, and keep moving.

There's a reframe that's genuinely useful here: stop evaluating decisions by their outcomes and start evaluating them by their process. A decision made carefully, from clear values and honest information, is a good decision, even if the result is disappointing. A decision made primarily to avoid accountability, to keep others comfortable, or to stay hidden in safety is a poor decision, even if it happens to produce a fine outcome.

Outcome-based evaluation of decisions creates a distorted feedback loop. Process-based evaluation creates a very different relationship with risk: one where the quality of your decision-making is something you can build, measure, and trust.

It also helps to look backward at your history with decisions you considered 'wrong' at the time. Most people who do this honestly discover that their supposedly worst decisions were often the most formative ones, the ones that redirected them toward something better, that taught them something essential, that proved they could handle more than they believed. That history is evidence. Use it.

Building Your Decision Muscle

Self-trust builds through accumulated evidence. You need a track record that proves, to yourself, that you can make decisions, handle outcomes, learn and adjust, and keep going. That track record doesn't arrive as a gift. You build it, deliberately, over time.

The principle is straightforward: start small. Make low-stakes decisions without seeking input. Notice how it feels. Then make slightly higher-stakes decisions the same way. The discomfort doesn't go away entirely, but your tolerance for it increases because you have evidence that you've been here before and it was fine.

Think of it as a progressive training program. You wouldn't walk into a gym after years away and immediately attempt a heavy lift. You'd start with manageable weights, build consistency, and gradually increase the load as your capacity develops. Decision-making without permission works the same way.

In the early weeks, the decisions can be genuinely small: choose a restaurant without consulting anyone. Book a trip without running it by someone first. Reply to an email with your own position rather than hedging. These feel trivial, and in isolation they are. But the practice they're building is not trivial at all. You are training your brain to experience making a decision, surviving it, and moving forward, without the detour through someone else's approval.

As weeks pass and the small decisions accumulate, you'll notice something shift. Not dramatic confidence, more like a quiet settling. A growing sense that your judgment is reliable. That you can handle outcomes you didn't predict. That the discomfort of deciding is manageable. That settling is the foundation on which genuine self-trust is built.

Reviewing the Record You're Building

At some point—after a week, after thirty days, after whatever feels like a natural pause—it's worth looking back at the decisions you've made and asking yourself what the record shows.

Not 'did everything go perfectly?' It almost certainly didn't. The question is: what kind of decision-maker is emerging in this record? Someone who acts on her own judgment. Someone who handles uncertain outcomes and adjusts. Someone who doesn't need the loop to move forward. Someone who owns her choices, including the ones that didn't go as planned.

That's the identity this chapter is building toward. Not someone who makes perfect decisions. Someone who has stopped waiting for permission to make them.

As you look back, also notice this: the decisions you were most afraid to make without permission, how many of them turned out to be survivable? How many produced outcomes that were within your range to handle? How many were actually less risky than they felt from inside the loop? The evidence almost always outpaces the fear. The fear was calibrated for someone who couldn't trust herself. The evidence belongs to someone who can.

Moving Forward

This week, use the decision framework on something you've been postponing. Not a small test run, but an actual decision you've been avoiding. Work through each step. Set your deadline. Make the call.

Alongside that, commit to thirty days of small daily decisions made without seeking external validation. One each day. Notice your reactions. Track what shifts. By the end of it, evaluate what the record proves about your actual decision-making ability—not the ability you fear is lacking, but the one you've been demonstrating all along.

Finally, look back at one past decision that didn't unfold as you expected. Ask what it taught you. Ask how you've used that learning. Ask what it proves about your ability to handle outcomes you didn't choose. The answer is almost always more than you've been giving yourself credit for.

The previous chapters of this book have been building a case: that you already have more than you've been exercising, that your resources are real, that your competence is documented. This chapter takes that case and makes it operational. Because recognizing your power and using it are two different things. The gap between them is closed one decision at a time.

Each decision you make without waiting for permission is a small act of identity consolidation. You are not becoming a different person, you are becoming more fully yourself. The version of you that has always been capable of leading her own life, who simply needed the practice of doing it to believe it.

That practice starts now. Not when it feels comfortable. Not when the loop has fully loosened its hold. Now, with the discomfort present, with the uncertainty intact, with the outcome unknown. That's always been the condition under which real decisions get made. You've always been capable of this. The difference is that now you've proved it to yourself.

CHAPTER 5

Your Internal Scorecard

Measuring Progress on Your Own Terms

— —

One of the hardest shifts in self-leadership is learning to validate your own progress without waiting for external recognition.

We're conditioned to look outward for proof that we're doing well: promotions, likes, compliments, awards, recognition. When those don't come, we assume we're failing, even when we're genuinely progressing.

This chapter is about building an internal validation system that doesn't depend on other people's approval.

Most people abandon progress not because they lack ability but because silence feels like failure. When recognition does not arrive on schedule, doubt fills the gap. This is not a confidence issue. It is a measurement issue.

If you do not define how progress is measured, you will default to public response as your metric. And public response is erratic, delayed, and often entirely unrelated to the quality of your work.

This is worth sitting with for a moment, because it reframes the problem entirely. The women who struggle most with self-validation are not, in most cases, women who lack self-awareness or motivation. They are women who are working hard, making real progress, and then looking up and finding no mirror to confirm what they've done. The work is real. The absence of confirmation makes it feel unreal.

The solution is not to care less about recognition, that's neither realistic nor useful. The solution is to build a validation system that operates independently of other people's attention. One that you control, that reflects your actual values, and that gives you reliable signal about whether you're moving in the right direction, whether anyone else notices or not.

That system doesn't arrive pre-built. It requires deliberate construction. This chapter walks you through how.

Why External Validation Fails

1. **Unreliable:** Other people are busy, distracted, and dealing with their own lives. You can't make people notice or care.
2. **Uncontrollable:** Recognition comes long after the work, and sometimes it's absent entirely.

3. **Delayed:** Great work goes unnoticed for reasons that have nothing to do with its quality.
4. **Absent:** If you're waiting for external validation to know you're on track, you're outsourcing your sense of progress to people who may never provide it.

If you're waiting for external validation to know you're on track, you're outsourcing your sense of progress to people who may never provide it.

There's a deeper problem with external validation that goes beyond its unreliability: even when it does arrive, it doesn't reliably tell you what you need to know. Praise from the wrong source reinforces the wrong behavior. Recognition for one thing can mask stagnation in another. Validation that arrives for how you present yourself rather than what you've built can quietly steer you away from the work that matters most.

External validation also has a ceiling effect on ambition. When your sense of progress depends on other people's responses, you unconsciously calibrate your goals to what's visible and legible to them. The ambitious, long-horizon work, the kind that doesn't produce visible results for months or years, becomes harder to sustain without internal measures to confirm you're on track.

None of this means that recognition is worthless. It can be genuinely useful information, and receiving it gracefully is its own skill. But receiving validation well is very different from needing it in order to continue. The goal here is independence, not indifference.

REAL STORY

Rachel started something quietly. A new initiative at work. A project she had been thinking about for months. She didn't announce it. She didn't ask for permission. She simply began. There was no applause. No immediate feedback. No visible reaction. Within days, she assumed it wasn't working. Nothing had gone wrong. No one had criticized it. But the absence of recognition felt like evidence of failure.

For weeks, she considered pulling back. Scaling it down. Waiting until someone noticed before investing more energy. Instead, she kept going. A month later, a senior colleague referenced the project in a meeting. Two months in, the results were measurable. What had felt invisible was quietly compounding. Impact and recognition rarely move at the same speed. Progress compounds internally long before it becomes visible externally.

Rachel's story is instructive not because it ended with recognition, though it did, but because of what would have happened if she'd stopped. The work itself was sound. The results were accumulating. The only thing threatening to derail it was the noise of silence.

This is the pattern worth learning to recognize. The impulse to pull back, scale down, or wait for someone to notice before investing more, that impulse is almost never a response to evidence that something isn't working. It's a response to the absence of confirmation. Learning to distinguish between those two things is one of the most practically valuable skills this book can give you.

Auditing Where You're Seeking Validation

Before you can build an internal validation system, it helps to see clearly where you've been relying on external ones. Most of us have specific domains, particular kinds of work or effort, where we reflexively look outward for confirmation.

Ask yourself: whose approval am I currently waiting for? What do I believe that approval would give me? And what evidence already exists that I'm progressing, regardless of whether anyone has acknowledged it?

The second question is often the most revealing: what do I believe that approval would give me? The honest answers tend to cluster around a few things. Certainty that the effort is worth continuing. Permission to take up space. Proof that you're not deluding yourself about your own capability. Reassurance that the people whose opinion you value see what you're building.

These are real needs. They're not signs of weakness or insecurity; they're the natural results of building something in conditions that don't offer much feedback. The question is whether those needs are best met by waiting for someone else to address them, or whether you can build systems that address them yourself.

The third question, what evidence already exists, is where most people underestimate themselves most significantly. Because the evidence is almost always there. Decisions that were made and held. Work that was completed. Challenges that were navigated. Small things that don't feel worth counting but collectively represent a pattern of capability. The audit is about making that evidence visible so it can function as the confirmation you've been waiting for someone else to provide.

Building Your Internal Scorecard

An internal scorecard tracks what matters to you, not what impresses others.

If you do not build your own scorecard, you inherit one. And inherited scorecards are built on comparison, visibility, and noise—metrics that were designed for someone else's life and someone else's definition of success.

An internal system measures alignment, consistency, skill development, resilience, and execution. These indicators are quieter, but far more predictive of long-term outcomes than the external signals most of us have been trained to track.

Building your own scorecard requires two things: knowing what matters to you, and being honest enough to measure it.

The first part sounds straightforward but often isn't. Many women discover, when they sit down to define their own metrics, that they've been pursuing goals that belong to someone else, a parent's definition of achievement, a profession's standard of success, a social group's measure of a life well lived. Defining your own scorecard forces that question into the open: is this what I'm actually building toward, or is this what I've absorbed as the thing I should be building toward?

The second part, honest measurement, requires resisting the temptation to set metrics that are primarily about how things look rather than how they're developing. Professional growth measured by title and salary is external. Professional growth measured by the complexity of problems you can now handle, the quality of your judgment, the breadth of your capability, that's internal. Both are real, but only one is fully yours to track.

Defining Your Success Metrics

Create your internal scorecard by identifying what truly indicates progress in your life. The categories below are a starting point, adjust them to reflect what genuinely matters in your particular situation.

Professional Growth

Society's default metric here is title, salary, and status. Your internal metric might be something different: the quality of problems you're being asked to solve, your confidence in your own expertise, the degree to which your work reflects your actual values, the skills you've added in the last six months. Define what progress looks like for you in your professional life, independent of how it would appear to someone on the outside.

Personal Development

This is perhaps the category most vulnerable to borrowed metrics, personal development is saturated with external benchmarks. Your internal metric here should reflect the specific areas you've identified as worth growing in. Not what a good person in your position should be developing, but what you've decided you want to become better at, and why.

Relationships

Relationship success is often measured externally by status, duration, or conventional milestones. Internally, the more useful metrics tend to be about quality: the honesty present in your closest relationships, your ability to maintain boundaries that reflect your actual values, the degree to which the people around you know and respect who you are rather than who you perform yourself to be.

Health and Energy

This is one of the areas where external metrics, appearance, weight, fitness benchmarks, most aggressively colonize internal experience. Your internal metric here might focus instead on energy levels, sleep quality, your relationship with your own body, the sustainability of how you're living. Progress that comes at the cost of your physical wellbeing is not progress by a well-built internal scorecard.

Financial Stability

Financial progress is often measured against what others appear to have or against abstract aspirational targets. A more useful internal metric tracks your relationship with money: the degree to which your spending reflects your values, the direction of travel in your financial security, your growing capacity to make financial decisions from a position of knowledge rather than anxiety.

As you define these metrics, notice which ones feel genuinely yours and which feel like they've been handed to you. You're allowed to adopt inherited metrics if they align with what you want: the point isn't to reject everything conventional. The point is to choose consciously, so that the scorecard you're playing against is one you've endorsed.

The act of writing these metrics down matters more than most people expect. Something that lives as a vague feeling of 'what I'm aiming for' is very difficult to measure against. Something written down becomes real enough to compare your actual life to. That comparison, honest and private, is the foundation of internal validation.

The Weekly Practice of Validating Yourself

Once a week, validate your own progress. Not in a performative way, this isn't a gratitude practice or a self-congratulation exercise. It's a perceptual recalibration.

The practice is simple: identify three things you accomplished, one way you showed up for yourself, and one challenge you handled. Do this for four weeks and observe what shifts.

The purpose of the weekly check-in is not to generate positive feelings, though it often does. The purpose is to correct a perceptual bias that most women share: the tendency to discount completed work immediately and focus attention almost entirely on what remains undone.

This bias is particularly insidious because it looks like drive. It presents as high standards, as ambition, as the refusal to be complacent. And in small doses, that orientation is genuinely useful. But when it becomes the dominant mode, when the ratio of noticing-what-you've-done to noticing-what-remains is badly skewed toward the latter, it creates a lived experience of perpetual inadequacy that has nothing to do with your actual performance.

The weekly check-in rebalances that ratio deliberately. When you systematically document what you've accomplished, how you've shown up, and what you've navigated, you are training your brain to register completed work as real. That registration is what external validation provides when it arrives. You're building the capacity to provide it yourself.

'One challenge you handled' deserves particular attention. Challenges handled are almost never counted by people who handled them, because handling them required effort that, in retrospect, feels like it should have been obvious or easy. It wasn't. The difficulty you worked through this week is evidence of your capability—specifically, the kind of capability that doesn't show up in highlight reels but forms the actual substance of a capable life. Counting it is not vanity. It is accuracy.

Moving Forward

This week, audit where you're seeking external approval and trace what you believe it would give you. Then start defining your own success metrics across the areas of your life that matter most to you, not society's benchmarks, but yours.

Alongside that, begin the weekly check-in practice. One consistent weekly habit of documenting what you've accomplished, how you showed up, and what you navigated. Keep it private if that makes it more honest. Sustain it for four weeks and assess what's shifted in how you read your own progress.

The shift this chapter is building toward is subtle but structural: from seeking confirmation to confirming yourself. That's not a small change. For many women, it represents a complete reorganization of how progress feels, from something that happens when someone else notices, to something that's present in the work itself, in the decisions made, in the effort sustained.

That reorganization doesn't happen all at once. It accumulates through practice, through weeks of deliberate self-measurement that gradually make the internal signal strong enough to stand on its own. At some point, the absence of external recognition stops feeling like evidence of failure and starts feeling neutral: information about other people's attention, not about your progress.

That's the destination. It doesn't require that you stop valuing recognition or that you become indifferent to how others see your work. It requires that you stop needing it to continue. Self-leadership that depends on external confirmation is, at its core, still waiting for rescue, just from a slightly different source. The version this book is building is one that runs on its own authority. This chapter is where that authority learns to sustain itself.

CHAPTER 6
Setting Boundaries Without Guilt

Protecting Your Time, Energy, and Decisions

— —

Self-leadership requires boundaries. But for many of us, setting boundaries triggers guilt, anxiety, or fear of disappointing others.

This chapter addresses how to protect your time, energy, and decisions without apologizing for it.

boundaries are not about control. They are about clarity. They define where your responsibility ends and someone else's begins.

Without boundaries, agency dissolves into accommodation. With boundaries, autonomy becomes visible.

It's worth being precise about what a boundary really is, because the word has accumulated enough cultural baggage to obscure its practical meaning. A boundary is not a wall. It is not a declaration of hostility or a rejection of the people around you. It is information, clear, honest information about what you are and aren't available for, what you will and won't do, what you are protecting and why.

Framed that way, boundaries are not fundamentally different from any other form of honest communication. The reason they feel different, the reason they generate guilt and anxiety in ways that other forms of honesty often don't, is that they require you to prioritize your own needs visibly. And for many women, that visibility feels dangerous. Not because it is, but because it has been learned as such, sometimes for very good historical and social reasons.

This chapter is about building the capacity to set boundaries steadily, not by eliminating the discomfort that precedes them, but by learning to act clearly despite it, and by accumulating enough evidence that the anticipated fallout rarely materializes.

Why Boundaries Feel Hard

Boundaries feel hard because they require saying no. And saying no often means disappointing someone, risking disapproval, claiming your needs matter, and facing potential conflict.

But without boundaries, you can't lead your life, you'll be living everyone else's agenda instead.

The discomfort that follows a boundary is often misinterpreted as wrongdoing. In reality, it is simply the nervous system adjusting to a new pattern.

Guilt does not always mean harm. Often, it simply means you are breaking a habit of over-accommodation.

The specific difficulty of boundaries for women who have been high-functioning accommodators deserves more than a passing acknowledgment, because it's more complicated than simply being 'too nice.' Many women who struggle to set boundaries are not passive people. They are often the most capable and relied-upon people in their professional and personal environments. The difficulty isn't lack of strength, it's that their strength has been consistently channeled into holding things together for others, and the social feedback they've received for doing so has been almost uniformly positive.

You get praised for being accommodating. You get called selfless, dependable, the one people can always count on. Those are genuinely good things, and the desire to be those things is not a flaw. The flaw, if it can be called that, is when the capacity to accommodate has no off switch, when every request lands as an obligation, when saying yes has become automatic and saying no requires a justification that satisfies not just the other person but an internal jury as well.

The guilt that follows a boundary in this pattern is not a signal that you've done something wrong. It's the sensation of breaking a deeply grooved habit. The nervous system has learned that accommodation equals safety, connection, and approval. When you decline to accommodate, it registers as a threat to those things, and produces a corresponding feeling. That feeling is real, but it is not accurate information about the situation. It is information about the habit.

The practical implication is this: guilt, when it follows a reasonable boundary, is not a reason to retract. It is a signal that the boundary is new, not that it is wrong.

REAL STORY

Maya had a reputation among her friends for being loving and supportive, which meant always available. Late night emotional debriefs. Girls' nights out. Weekend favors. She rarely said no. When she started her own business, she began protecting her time, declining spontaneous weekend plans and limiting late-night calls.

She felt immediate guilt. She imagined resentment building. Nothing dramatic happened. A few friends adjusted. One pushed back once. Most simply adapted. What changed was not the friendships. It was Maya's energy. The relationships became clearer. The guilt faded as consistency replaced apology.

Maya's experience follows a pattern that repeats across almost every account of someone learning to set boundaries after a long period of over-accommodation. The internal experience, the guilt, the anticipated fallout, the rehearsed justifications, is almost always more dramatic than what happens externally. This isn't because other people don't notice. They do. It's because most people, when someone they care about begins to operate with greater clarity about their own capacity, eventually respect it. They may test it first. But they recalibrate.

Where You Need Boundaries

Before you can set a boundary, you need to know where one is missing. Most people who struggle with boundaries have them in some areas and not others, the pattern is rarely uniform. Looking at the specific domains of your life is more useful than a general sense that you 'need to be better at saying no.'

With Family

Family boundaries are often the hardest, because the relationships are the oldest and the patterns are the most deeply grooved. The dynamics that were established before you had any real agency—who you were expected to be, what you were expected to give, how conflict was managed—can reassert themselves with startling force in adult life, even when you've built a very different sense of yourself everywhere else. If you find that you consistently revert to a younger, less autonomous version of yourself in family contexts, the boundaries you're missing there are likely the most important ones to identify.

With Friends

Friendship boundaries tend to center on availability and reciprocity. Are there people in your life who consistently take more than they give, whose crises become your urgencies, whose needs reliably displace your own? Are there relationships where you've been so consistently accommodating that the other person has no real sense of your actual limits? The question isn't whether these relationships are worth keeping. It's whether they're currently operating on terms that reflect who you truly are.

At Work

Professional boundaries are often the most socially complex because the power dynamics are real and the consequences of getting it wrong can feel genuinely costly. But the absence of professional boundaries is also genuinely costly, in ways that accumulate more slowly and therefore feel less urgent until they don't. Scope creep, availability expectations that extend well beyond working hours, decisions being made over your head in areas that are yours to own, these are not small inconveniences. They are the steady erosion of the professional authority you've built.

With Yourself

Self-directed boundaries, commitments you make to yourself and then override, standards you set and then quietly lower, promises about your own time and energy that you consistently break, are worth taking as seriously as boundaries with other people. Every time you override a commitment to yourself in favor of someone else's request, you are reinforcing the belief that your own needs are negotiable in a way that other people's are not. That belief compounds. The capacity to hold a boundary with someone else is closely related to the capacity to hold one with yourself.

The Language of Boundaries

Clear language reduces friction. You do not need elaborate explanations. You need consistency.

The examples below are not scripts to memorize. They illustrate tone, direct, calm, and final. The goal is not to sound a particular way; it's to be clear enough that there is no ambiguity about your position, and steady enough that pushback doesn't move you.

1. When someone asks for your time:

"I'd love to help, but I don't have bandwidth right now."

This phrasing is useful because it's honest without being explanatory. You're not citing a specific competing commitment, which invites negotiation around whether that commitment is important enough, you're naming your capacity. "I don't have bandwidth" is a complete statement. It doesn't require a reason, and it doesn't leave a gap for "what if I helped you make space?" The "I'd love to help" opener softens the delivery without diluting the message, use it if it's genuine, skip it if it isn't.

2. When you need to protect your decision:

"I've thought about this carefully and I'm committed to this choice."

This one is specifically for the situation where someone is pressuring you to revisit a decision you've already made, not offering new information, but simply expressing displeasure or repeating their original objection. The phrasing signals two things: that you took the decision seriously (which forecloses the "you haven't really thought this through" angle), and that the decision is settled (which forecloses "if I just keep pushing, she'll eventually change her mind"). It's not defensive. It's conclusive.

3. When someone criticizes your boundary:

"I understand this is different from what you expected. This is what works for me."

Acknowledgment without capitulation. The first sentence validates that something has shifted, you're not gaslighting anyone about the change. The second sentence re-anchors in your own position without justifying it. What this phrasing deliberately avoids is the impulse to explain why the boundary is reasonable, which typically opens a negotiation about whether your reasons are sufficient. Your reasons don't need to meet someone else's threshold for sufficiency. The boundary is yours. "This is what works for me" is both true and complete.

4. When you need to decline without explanation:

"Thank you for thinking of me, but I'm going to pass."

This is the one most people find hardest, because it doesn't offer a reason, and the absence of a reason feels rude, or at least uncomfortable. It isn't. You are not obligated to justify every choice you make about your own time and energy. In fact, the habit of always offering reasons for declining is part of what keeps many women trapped in accommodation, because reasons can always be argued with. Sometimes 'I'm going to pass' is the complete and honest answer.

5. When someone pushes back:

"I hear you, and my answer is still no."

Possibly the most important phrase in this chapter. Pushback is the test. It's the moment that determines whether your boundary was real or whether it was an opening position. 'I hear you' is not agreement, it's acknowledgment. It signals that you've registered what they've said and it hasn't changed your answer. 'My answer is still no' closes the loop without hostility and without further explanation. The word 'still' is doing significant work here: it communicates that the pushback has been received and considered and that it hasn't moved the needle. That's the message you need to send.

Building the Practice

Repetition builds tolerance. The first boundary feels disruptive. The tenth feels normal.

Tracking is not about performance. It is about noticing that the anticipated fallout rarely materializes. When you begin paying deliberate attention to what happens after you set a boundary, as opposed to what you feared would happen, you start accumulating evidence that your nervous system can draw on the next time.

For a month, notice each time you set a boundary. Note how you felt: guilty, empowered, anxious, or relieved. Then note what actually happened. This last part is the most important, because it's where the evidence lives.

What most people discover when they track this honestly is a significant gap between anticipated consequences and actual ones. The friend who was 'definitely going to be upset' was fine, or briefly upset but moved on quickly. The colleague who 'wouldn't respect it' respected it. The family member who 'would make it into a big thing' made it into a smaller thing than expected, or a brief thing, or nothing at all.

This doesn't mean pushback never happens, sometimes it does, and that's worth noting too. But even when it does, tracking helps you see that you survived it. That you held the boundary anyway. That the relationship continued. The record of your own resilience in the face of pushback is evidence that your capacity is greater than the anxiety suggests.

Over time, this practice does something more structural than just building a habit. It changes the story you tell yourself about who you are in relation to other people's needs. From 'someone who can't say no' to 'someone who is learning to be clear about her capacity.' From 'someone who prioritizes everyone else first' to 'someone whose own needs are part of the picture.' Those identity shifts don't come from insight alone. They come from a record of behavior that proves the new story true.

Moving Forward

This week, audit where you're missing boundaries, across family, friends, work, and your commitments to yourself. You don't need to address all of them at once. Choose one domain where the cost of the missing boundary is most visible, and identify one specific boundary to set within it.

Use the language in this chapter as a starting point, adjusted to your own voice. The tone matters more than the exact words: direct, calm, and final. Not apologetic. Not over-explained. Clear.

Track what happens. Not just how you felt, but what actually occurred. The evidence that accumulates over a month of consistent practice will do more to reduce guilt than any amount of reasoning about why the guilt is misplaced.

The goal is not to eliminate guilt immediately. The goal is to act despite it. This distinction matters enormously, because many people wait to set boundaries until they feel comfortable doing so, until the guilt has subsided, until they feel certain, until the timing feels right. That wait can be indefinite. The guilt doesn't lift before the action. It lifts because of it.

boundaries do not require hostility. They require steadiness. Each boundary held, each pushback navigated, each feared consequence that fails to materialize is a small deposit into the account of your own credibility with yourself. Over time, that account grows large enough to act from without consulting the guilt first.

CHAPTER 7

Building Daily Self-Leadership Habits

Consolidating Identity Through Daily Evidence

— —

Self-leadership isn't a one-time decision. It's a practice built through daily habits that compound over time.

This chapter focuses on the small, repeated actions that transform how you show up for yourself.

Self-leadership is reinforced through evidence. Each small action becomes proof that you are directing your own life rather than reacting to it.

The goal is not productivity but identity consolidation. When actions align with decisions, trust strengthens.

This distinction, between productivity and identity consolidation, is worth dwelling on, because it changes what you're trying to build here. A productivity framework asks: how much did I accomplish?

An identity consolidation framework asks: did I act like the person I'm choosing to become?

The previous chapters of this book have built a case for who that person is. She recognizes when she's waiting for rescue and chooses differently. She acts on the authority and power she already has rather than waiting to be given more. She measures her progress against her own standards, sets boundaries without excessive apology, and makes decisions without routing them through everyone else's approval first.

The habits in this chapter are not about becoming that person. You have already been becoming her—through the recognition, the inventory, the decisions made, the boundaries held, the validation earned. The habits are about consolidating her. About making the new patterns the default rather than the effortful exception. That's what daily practice does: it drives the new neural grooves deeper until they run on their own.

The Power of Micro-Habits

You don't need dramatic overhauls. You need consistent small actions that prove to yourself, daily, that you're leading your life.

Small Action → Repetition → Evidence → Self-Trust → Identity Consolidation

Examples of self-leadership micro-habits:

1. Making one decision without seeking permission.
2. Honoring one boundary.

3. Validating one small win.
4. Taking one action on your own terms.
5. Saying no to one thing that doesn't serve you.

The reason micro-habits work, and the reason dramatic overhauls usually don't, is that the brain changes through repetition, not through resolution. A single powerful moment of clarity is meaningful, but it doesn't rewire anything on its own. What rewires the pattern is the accumulated weight of many small moments, each one a minor instance of choosing differently from the way you used to default.

There's also something important about the scale. A small, daily act of self-direction is achievable on almost any day, including the difficult ones, the overwhelmed ones, the ones where everything else feels like too much. A large, ambitious habit requires conditions that good days provide and bad days don't. The micro-habit has none of that fragility. It asks only for a few minutes and one deliberate choice. And on the days when everything feels hard, one deliberate choice is exactly the kind of evidence the nervous system needs to register that the new pattern is still intact.

Over weeks and months, these small acts accumulate into something that isn't small at all: a consistent record of a person who acts from her own authority. That record is what self-trust is actually built from. Not the intention to lead yourself. The evidence that you do.

REAL STORY

Elena decided that every day she would make one small decision without consulting anyone, apologizing or over-explaining. Sometimes it was minor, choosing to take a full lunch break and walk to the park alone instead of eating at her desk and 'multitasking'. Sometimes it was larger, declining a late meeting request in order to be home in time for dinner with her family.

At first, the actions felt small. But within weeks, she noticed something shift. When her manager asked for her recommendation on a project approach, she gave it directly instead of presenting two options and waiting to see which one he preferred. Decisions became easier. boundaries required less rehearsal. The habit of checking outward weakened. The change did not come from a dramatic breakthrough. It came from repetition.

What Elena's experience captures is the mechanism that sits beneath all the work in this book: the habit of checking outward. That habit—the reflexive look to someone else for confirmation before acting, the internal question of 'is this okay?' that precedes so many decisions, is not eliminated through insight. It weakens through practice. Each time you make a decision without running it past someone first, the checking reflex has slightly less pull. Each time you decline without over-explaining, the need to justify yourself becomes slightly less urgent. The habit doesn't vanish. It simply, over time, loses its grip.

The other thing worth noting in Elena's story is the sequence: the actions felt insignificant first, and then the shift became visible. This is almost always how it works. The change is happening before you can see it. The evidence accumulates beneath the surface until there's enough of it to register. If you stop before that threshold you'll never get to see what the consistency would have built. Elena got there by staying with it past the point where it felt like it was working.

The Morning Routine: Setting Direction

A morning routine is not about optimization. It is about direction.

The first minutes of your day set the tone for who is leading. Instead of designing something elaborate, choose one deliberate action that signals authorship. It might be deciding your top priority before checking your phone. It might be reviewing one boundary you intend to honor today. It might be choosing the pace of your morning rather than reacting to it.

The action itself matters less than the message it sends: I lead this day.

Keep it short. Keep it consistent. Let the repetition build identity.

The specific enemy of a useful morning routine is what happens when you begin the day in reactive mode, responding to messages, notifications, and other people's urgencies before you've established your own footing. When the first twenty minutes of your day are spent attending to external demands, you've begun the day in a posture of response rather than direction. That posture tends to persist.

What a brief morning practice does is insert a moment of agency before the reactive mode begins. It doesn't have to be long. Five minutes is enough to establish the pattern. The question it's implicitly answering is: whose agenda does this day begin with? When the answer is consistently yours, you're building a daily piece of evidence that you are someone who leads her own mornings, and by extension, her own days.

One practical suggestion: decide your one most important thing for the day before you look at anyone else's requests. Not a full task list, just one thing that, if you accomplished nothing else, would represent a day where you moved something meaningful forward. The act of identifying that thing from your own priorities, before you've been pulled into other people's, is itself a small act of self-direction. It takes two minutes. It signals to yourself, first thing, that your priorities exist and that you're attending to them.

The Evening Reflection: Gathering Evidence

Evening reflection is not evaluation. It is evidence gathering.

At the end of each day, take a few minutes to notice:

1. One decision you made without outsourcing approval.
2. One boundary you honored.
3. One moment you acted in alignment with who you're choosing to be.

This is not about perfection. It is about pattern recognition.

Most people underestimate how quickly identity consolidates when evidence is acknowledged daily. What you notice, you reinforce.

Morning establishes direction. Evening establishes evidence. Together, they create a feedback loop of self-trust.

The reason to frame this as evidence gathering rather than evaluation is important: evaluation tends toward judgment and judgment tends toward the question of whether you did enough. That question rarely has a satisfying answer, and it reliably shifts focus toward what's missing rather than what's present. The evening reflection is not trying to assess whether you had a good enough day. It's trying to register what really happened.

The three prompts, decision made autonomously, boundary honored, moment of alignment, are chosen deliberately because they map directly to the habits this book has been building. They're not general productivity markers. They're specific to the identity you're consolidating. A day in which you noticed one of each is a day in which the new pattern ran. That's the only standard being applied.

There's a compounding dimension to this practice that becomes more visible over time. In the early weeks, they may feel small, a minor decision, a gentle no, a moment of noticing. But as they accumulate, they become a record. And a record of someone who consistently makes autonomous decisions, consistently honors boundaries, and consistently notices when she's acting in alignment, that record describes someone whose identity is no longer tentative. It describes someone who has arrived.

Habit Stacking: Attaching Agency to What You Already Do

Self-leadership strengthens when attached to existing behavior.

Rather than adding new routines to an already full day, attach one act of agency to something you already do consistently. After brushing your teeth, choose your primary decision for the day. After closing your laptop, acknowledge one aligned action. After pouring your morning coffee, review one boundary you intend to protect today.

The principle is simple: link autonomy to repetition. Over time, the existing cue itself becomes a trigger for self-leadership.

The Compounding Effect

The transformation does not happen in a single morning.

It happens quietly. One decision. One boundary. One reflection. Then another. The brain begins to register consistency. Doubt softens. The urge to check outward weakens. Identity stabilizes.

Repetition builds proof. Proof builds trust. Trust becomes authority.

Compounding is a concept most commonly applied to finance, but it operates in exactly the same way in identity. A small daily deposit—one autonomous decision, one held boundary, one moment of self-validation—doesn't look like much in isolation. The first week of deposits is barely visible. The second week, the same. But the deposits don't disappear. They accumulate. And at some point, usually somewhere in the four-to-eight-week range for most people, the accumulated evidence reaches a threshold at which something perceptibly shifts.

The shift tends to show up not as a dramatic change but as an absence. The absence of the reflexive question 'is this okay?' before making a routine decision. The absence of the long internal debate before declining something you don't want to do. The absence of the anxious wait for someone else to confirm that your instinct was right. These things don't vanish entirely, but they lose their automatic quality. They become occasional rather than constant. And in that change—quiet, gradual, built from nothing more dramatic than daily small actions—is the substance of what this book has been building toward.

You do not arrive at self-leadership through a single decision or a single powerful chapter. You arrive through the accumulated weight of choosing, day after day, to act from your own authority. The habits in this chapter are the vehicle. The destination is a version of yourself for whom self-direction is no longer an effort but a default, someone who has moved so far from the waiting room that she can barely remember what it felt like to need permission to begin.

Moving Forward

Choose one daily act that signals leadership to yourself. Keep it small. Keep it steady. Anchor it to something you already do.

Design a brief morning practice, five to ten minutes, that begins your day with direction rather than reaction. Identify your one most important thing before you open anyone else's messages.

At the end of each day, notice one aligned action. Not whether you did everything. One thing you did that proves the new pattern ran.

The question this chapter leaves you with is not whether you feel ready to lead your life. That question has a moving target for an answer, and waiting for the feeling of readiness is one of the central patterns this book has been dismantling from the first page.

The question is simpler and more immediate: did you act like you were leading it today? One small decision made on your own authority. One boundary held. One moment noticed. That's all a single day requires. And a life built from days like that is not a life spent waiting for rescue. It is a life directed, imperfectly, sometimes messily, but genuinely and increasingly from the inside out.

The next chapter addresses what happens when the old patterns surface again, because they will. Not as evidence that the work wasn't real, but as a normal feature of the consolidation process. Knowing how to move through those moments, rather than being derailed by them, is the final piece of the practice this book is building.

CHAPTER 8

When Old Patterns Return

Recognition, Recovery and Returning to Authority

— —

Old patterns will return.

You'll catch yourself waiting for permission again. Seeking validation. Doubting your authority. Postponing decisions.

This is not failure. This is familiarity.

Growth does not erase the past. It builds new patterns alongside old ones. Under stress, the mind often reaches for what it practiced longest.

The return of an old pattern is not evidence that you've lost progress. It is evidence that the pattern was once deeply practiced.

The question is not whether it returns. The question is how quickly you notice.

This reframe, from 'what went wrong?' to 'how quickly did I notice?', is one of the most practically useful shifts in this entire book. It changes the relationship with regression from one of shame and self-judgment to one of information and response. When the question is 'what went wrong?', the answer tends to be an indictment. When the question is 'how quickly did I notice?', the answer is a measurement: one you can improve on.

There's also something important about naming what a pattern return is and isn't. It is not evidence that the growth was superficial, not proof that the old identity was more real than the new one, not a sign that you're incapable of sustained change. It is a feature of how the brain consolidates new learning: under pressure or in familiar high-activation environments, older, more practiced patterns temporarily reassert themselves. That's normal. It doesn't mean permanent. It means the new grooves aren't yet deep enough to hold under all conditions, which is precisely what continued practice is for.

This chapter prepares you for that pattern, not as an exception to growth, but as a predictable part of it, and gives you a simple, reliable way to move through it quickly when it arrives.

Why Patterns Return

Old patterns return because they're deeply grooved. You've practiced them for years, maybe decades. They're your brain's default when you're stressed or overwhelmed, facing major uncertainty, triggered by specific people or situations, exhausted or depleted, or emotionally activated in ways that feel familiar.

Under pressure, your brain reaches for what's familiar, even if it no longer serves you.

Returning to old patterns doesn't erase your progress. Your new neural pathways still exist. You just temporarily defaulted to the old ones. You can switch back.

The specific mechanism is worth understanding, because it changes how you interpret the experience. The brain doesn't delete old patterns when new ones are built. Both exist simultaneously, the old groove and the new one. Under normal conditions, with sufficient resources and without significant pressure, the newer pattern runs because it's the more recently practiced one. But when resources drop—through stress, fatigue, emotional activation, or environmental familiarity—the brain's efficiency systems kick in and reach for the deepest groove. The deepest groove is almost always the old one.

This is why certain environments are reliably activating in ways that feel disproportionate to their actual stakes. A family home where you spent twenty years learning to defer carries more pattern-activation potential than almost any new environment, regardless of how much you've changed. It isn't that the environment is more powerful than you. It's that it's running older, more practiced code. Once you know that, you can prepare for it rather than being blindsided by it.

The reframe that makes this actionable is the shift from 'why am I back here?' to 'how quickly did I notice?' Recovery speed is the real metric. Not whether the pattern appeared, it will, but how long it ran before you caught it. That gap shrinks with practice. In the early stages of building new patterns, you might not notice for days. Later, you notice within hours. Eventually, you notice mid-sentence. That progression is growth, even when it doesn't feel like it.

Getting Stuck vs. Returning

There are two paths when a pattern resurfaces.

Getting stuck looks like this: the pattern returns, you don't notice, days pass, the old narrative regains control, and discouragement sets in, which makes it harder to act, which allows the pattern to deepen further.

Returning looks different: the pattern returns, you notice, you name it calmly, you make one aligned decision, and you re-establish authority.

The slip is not the problem. Delay is. Every time you shorten the gap between awareness and correction, you strengthen identity.

The discouragement spiral in the 'getting stuck' path deserves specific attention, because it has its own momentum. Once you've been in an old pattern long enough to notice it, the awareness itself often arrives with a heavy narrative attached: I've lost all my progress. I knew this wouldn't last. I'm back to square one. That narrative is not an accurate description of the situation. It's an old story that the activated pattern is generating. And if you act from that story, if you treat it as evidence rather than as noise, you will make decisions from a diminished place, which produces diminished results, which seems to confirm the story.

The interruption is simple but requires deliberateness: don't let the narrative run. Name what's happened: an old pattern surfaced in a high-activation situation, and move directly to action. One decision. One boundary. The action doesn't need to be significant. It needs to be real. A real choice made from your own authority, however small, is the fastest way to interrupt the discouragement spiral because it produces immediate evidence that contradicts the 'back to square one' story.

REAL STORY

Lena had been practicing self-leadership for months. Decisions felt cleaner. boundaries felt steadier. Then she attended a family gathering. Within a day, she was asking her mother whether she thought she should take the job offer she had already decided to accept. She was volunteering to take on the holiday cooking because no one else had stepped forward and the silence felt like an accusation.

On the second evening, she recognized it. Nothing dramatic had happened. No confrontation. No collapse. Just an old pattern in a familiar environment, the same house, the same dynamics, the same unspoken rules she had grown up navigating. Instead of spiraling into self-criticism, she adjusted.

That night she told her mother simply that she had already made her decision about the job and was feeling good about it, and left it there. The next morning, she suggested they all divide the holiday cooking this year and she wouldn't be handling it alone, then didn't fill the silence that followed. No over-explanation. No performance of justification. The environment did not change. She did. That was enough.

What Lena's story illustrates with particular clarity is the scale of what was required to correct course. Not a dramatic act of reclamation. Not a confrontation or a declaration. Three small, deliberate choices: one decision made from her own authority, one boundary held, one refusal to over-explain. That's all it took to re-establish the pattern.

This is worth holding onto when a pattern return feels overwhelming. The correction almost never requires as much as the anxiety suggests. The anxious version of the situation generates elaborate plans for how to fix things, conversations to have, positions to assert, and changes to make. The practical version requires one aligned action. Then another. The pattern re-establishes itself through the same mechanism it was built through in the first place: repetition. A few deliberate repetitions of the new pattern, even in an activating environment, is enough to bring it back online.

The Early Signals

Pattern return rarely arrives dramatically. It shows up in the small, quiet behaviors that are easy to dismiss individually but reliable as a cluster: delaying a decision you could make now, seeking multiple opinions for reassurance rather than information, minimizing a recent win, abandoning a boundary you'd previously held, waiting to feel 'ready' before acting.

These are not crises. They are signals. The faster you recognize them, the easier they are to correct.

The reason these signals are easy to miss is that each one, in isolation, has a plausible innocent explanation. Delaying a decision is sometimes prudent. Seeking opinions is sometimes genuinely useful. Feeling uncertain before acting is sometimes appropriate caution. The pattern is visible not in any single behavior but in the cluster, several of these appearing together, or any one of them appearing in a domain where you'd previously been operating with more confidence.

There's also a specific signal worth naming that doesn't appear on the standard list: the impulse to over-explain. When you find yourself constructing elaborate justifications for choices that didn't previously require them, justifying a boundary to someone who didn't ask, over-explaining a decision to someone who didn't challenge it, that's a reliable indicator that the old need for external approval has been reactivated. The over-explanation is a bid for validation dressed as communication.

The fuller set of signals to watch for: postponing decisions that could be made now; seeking opinions before forming your own; waiting for someone else to act first; minimizing your own wins or capabilities; letting a boundary erode that you'd previously held; feeling vaguely powerless without a clear reason; catastrophizing about minor choices; over-explaining decisions that didn't require justification; reverting to agreement in conversations where you actually disagree. Three or more of these appearing together is enough to treat as a signal worth acting on.

The Return Loop

When you notice an old pattern reappearing, move through a simple sequence.

Notice it without judgment. Name it clearly, not as failure, but as activation: an old pattern running in a familiar context. Make one autonomous decision, however small. Reinforce one boundary. Acknowledge the correction.

That is all. You do not need a dramatic reset. You need one aligned action. Authority is restored through movement.

Each step in this sequence deserves a word on why it's there.

Noticing without judgment is the prerequisite for everything that follows. If the noticing arrives freighted with self-criticism, 'I can't believe I'm doing this again', it generates a defensive or shame-based response, neither of which produces clear action. Noticing without judgment means treating the observation as neutral information: a pattern surfaced. That's it. No verdict on your character, no projection into the future, no narrative about what it means.

Naming it clearly serves a specific function: it interrupts the automatic running of the pattern by making it conscious. An unconscious pattern runs itself. A named pattern requires a response. The naming doesn't need to be elaborate: 'I've been deferring to others in this environment' is sufficient. What matters is that you've moved from the pattern running you to you observing it. That shift in position is where agency becomes available again.

Making one autonomous decision is the pivot. It doesn't need to be large. It needs to be real—a genuine choice made from your own authority without routing it through someone else's approval. The act of making it is the message you're sending to yourself: the pattern doesn't control the outcome. You do. One real decision creates the evidence that makes the next one easier.

Reinforcing one boundary follows the same logic. In high-activation environments, boundaries tend to be the first thing to soften. Reasserting one, calmly, without over-explaining, is a direct signal that your capacity to protect your own position is intact.

Acknowledging the correction is the step most often skipped, and skipping it is a missed opportunity. You noticed. You named it. You acted. That sequence is self-leadership functioning correctly, not the absence of pattern activation, but the presence of a working response to it. Acknowledging it, even briefly and privately, registers the evidence in the place it matters most.

Preparing for High-Activation Situations

Some environments carry more history than others. Family dynamics, authority figures, major life transitions, and periods of sustained exhaustion are all reliably activating. Instead of hoping you'll respond differently when you arrive, decide in advance how you will.

Not a script. A stance. What version of you is entering this environment? What decision belongs to you? What boundary will you protect?

Preparation reduces surprise. It doesn't eliminate activation, nothing does, but it means the activation finds you with a position already established rather than having to construct one from scratch while the old pattern is running.

The preparation itself is brief. Before entering a situation you know to be activating, a family gathering, a performance review, a conversation with someone who reliably pulls old dynamics forward, spend a few minutes with three questions. What decisions are mine to make in this context, and which ones require someone else's input? What boundary am I most likely to let slide, and what would holding it look like? Who am I walking in as, the version shaped by this environment's history, or the version I've been building?

The third question is the most important one. Every high-activation environment carries an implicit invitation to revert to the person you were there before. The invitation isn't malicious; it's simply the gravity of shared history. The people in these environments have known you for a long time, and they have well-established expectations of who you are in relation to them. Those expectations can be a significant pull, not because you can't resist them but because they're operating constantly and mostly invisibly.

Naming in advance who you're choosing to be in this context is a form of pre-commitment. You're not guaranteeing perfect performance, no preparation does that. You're establishing a reference point to return to when the activation pulls you in another direction. That reference point is what makes the correction faster: instead of having to reconstruct your position from scratch, you're returning to a stance you already set.

Learning From Each Return

Every pattern return carries information. What triggered it? How quickly did you notice? What helped you correct? What will you do differently when this situation arises again?

This is not self-analysis for its own sake. It is calibration, the ongoing process of understanding your own activation conditions more precisely so that preparation becomes more targeted and recovery becomes faster over time.

The calibration loop looks like this: pattern surfaces, you notice, you correct, you extract the information. The extraction takes a few minutes and produces two things, a more precise understanding of your activation conditions, and evidence of your own recovery capacity.

The first is useful for preparation. If you discover that a specific person reliably activates a particular pattern, you can prepare for encounters with that person more specifically. If you discover that exhaustion is the common thread across multiple pattern returns, that's information about what conditions you need to protect in order to sustain the new pattern.

The second, the evidence of recovery capacity, is useful for the next time. One of the things that makes pattern returns feel destabilizing is the implicit fear that this time, you won't recover. That you'll stay in the old pattern. That the progress wasn't durable. The record of previous recoveries is the direct counter to that fear. You recovered last time. And the time before. The record isn't a guarantee, but it is evidence, the kind that weighs more than anxiety.

Progress, Not Perfection

Self-leadership is not the absence of regression. It is slipping less often, catching yourself faster, recovering more quickly, and remaining steadier under pressure than you did before.

You are not measured by whether the old pattern surfaces. You are measured by how quickly you return.

Old patterns may return. But they no longer control the outcome. That is the difference between where you started and where you are now, and it is not a small difference.

The standard this chapter is holding you to is worth naming explicitly, because it's easy to apply the wrong one. The wrong standard is: does the old pattern still surface? By that standard, you will appear to fail regularly, because the pattern will surface regularly, especially in high-activation conditions, for a long time. Neural grooves built over years don't disappear in months.

The right standard is: when it surfaces, what happens next? Does it run for weeks unnoticed, or do you catch it within a day? Do you spiral into discouragement, or do you make one aligned decision and move forward? Do you need external confirmation that you're on track, or do you have your own evidence to draw on? Those shifts, in speed of recognition, in quality of response, in source of authority, are the real indicators of progress. They're quieter than a dramatic transformation, but they're more durable.

Old patterns may return, but they no longer control the outcome. That phrase captures the actual destination. Not the elimination of old patterns. Not a life free from the pull of familiar dynamics. A life in which those patterns surface and you move through them, rather than being moved by them. A life directed from the inside out, reliably enough to be called yours.

Moving Forward

When you notice a pattern returning, act within the same day. Make one autonomous decision. Reassert one boundary. Acknowledge one aligned action.

Before entering any situation you know to be activating, spend a few minutes establishing your stance. Know what decisions are yours, what boundary you'll protect, and who you're choosing to be when the environment's gravity pulls in another direction.

After each recovery, extract the information. What triggered it, how quickly you noticed, what helped. That calibration is what makes the next one shorter.

CHAPTER 9

Money and Self-Leadership

Financial Autonomy as a Core Expression of Self-Leadership

— —

Of all the places the rescue fantasy takes root, money is one of the most fertile. It is the domain where capable women—women who negotiate contracts, manage teams, make complex decisions at work—will hand over the keys entirely. They wait for a partner who earns more. They wait for a raise that makes budgeting feel less painful. They wait for a windfall, an inheritance, a better job, a different life. They wait, in other words, for something external to change before they start taking charge of what is already theirs to lead.

This chapter is not about financial advice — no investment strategies, tax planning, or debt payoff formulas. Those conversations belong with a qualified financial professional. What this chapter is about is the pattern underneath the numbers: the habit of outsourcing authority over your financial life, and what it costs you when you do.

Money is where self-leadership becomes concrete. When you can see your numbers clearly, make decisions that reflect your actual values, and stop waiting for permission or rescue, you are not just managing your finances better. You are practicing the same muscle this entire book is about, the capacity to direct your own life from the inside out.

Why Money Feels Different

Money is not a neutral subject. It arrives in most of our lives already loaded, with family history, with shame, with power dynamics that were established long before we had any say in the matter. The way your parents talked about money (or didn't), the messages you absorbed about what people like you are supposed to have and want and deserve, the gender scripts around who manages finances and who defers—all of it is in the room every time you sit down with a bank statement.

This is why avoidance makes sense as a response, even when it doesn't serve you. Money is tied to survival and security in a way few other topics are. It is connected, often painfully, to self-worth, the sense that what you earn reflects your value as a person. It is loaded with social taboo: most of us find it easier to discuss our relationship history in detail than to tell a close friend what we make. And it is drenched in judgment, from others but more relentlessly from ourselves.

Add to that the fact that money is genuinely complex, and you have a recipe for a specific kind of paralysis: not the paralysis of someone who doesn't care, but the paralysis of someone who cares too much and feels too exposed to look directly at the reality. The avoidance isn't apathy. It's protection.

Understanding that doesn't mean staying in it. It means you can stop treating money avoidance as a character flaw and start treating it as a pattern—one you can interrupt, on purpose, starting now.

Financial autonomy doesn't mean being rich. It means being in the driver's seat of your financial life, knowing what's happening, making intentional choices, and not avoiding money out of fear or shame.

The Money Avoidance Pattern

The pattern looks different for different people, but it has a recognizable shape. At one end, there is the woman who simply doesn't look, who hasn't checked her account balance in weeks, who lets financial mail pile up unopened, who swipes her card and holds her breath. At the other end, there is the woman who has handed everything to someone else, a partner, a parent, an accountant, and told herself this is just practical, that she has more important things to focus on, that she was never good at this stuff anyway.

Both versions are avoidance. Both give away power. And both are far more common among capable, intelligent women than most people would guess, because the same sophistication that makes it easy to identify the problem also makes it easy to construct convincing explanations for why you're not dealing with it yet.

What avoidance costs you is not just money, though it often costs you that too. It costs you clarity. You cannot make good decisions about your career, about your relationships, about what risks you can afford to take when you don't know what you're working with. Avoidance keeps you in a state of vague, background anxiety, the kind where you're never quite sure if things are fine or terrible. That low-level dread is exhausting. And it keeps you dependent, because when you don't know your own numbers, you are always at least partly relying on hope rather than information.

The antidote to avoidance is not enthusiasm about spreadsheets. It's something simpler and more fundamental: the decision to look. Not to fix everything at once, not to have it all figured out, but to know what is actually there. Knowledge shifts the ground beneath you. Once you know the real number, whatever it is, you can make a real decision. You move from managing your anxiety to managing your finances, and those are very different activities.

REAL STORY

Lisa had been doing what she privately called 'magic thinking' with her bank account for the better part of two years. She knew roughly what she earned. She knew roughly what her fixed expenses were. Beyond that, she kept things deliberately vague, not checking balances, not reviewing her spending, operating on the assumption that if something was really wrong, she'd know. The anxiety was constant, but she'd learned to treat it as background noise.

The moment that changed things wasn't a financial crisis. It was a conversation with a colleague who mentioned, casually, that she'd just set up an automatic transfer to her savings account. 'I decided I needed to know what I have before I could plan anything,' her colleague said. Something in that sentence landed differently than Lisa expected.

> That night, she logged into her accounts. All of them. She wrote down every number she found. The experience was uncomfortable in the way she'd feared, but it wasn't the catastrophe she'd been bracing for. What she found was messy and imperfect, but it was also real, and real turned out to be something she could work with. The anxiety didn't disappear, but it changed shape. It stopped being dread and started being information. She knew what needed attention. She could make a plan. That was the shift: not from broke to wealthy, but from vague fear to specific agency.

Lisa's story illustrates something important: the thing you're avoiding is almost never as bad as the anxiety generated by not looking. Fear expands to fill the space avoidance creates. Once you remove the avoidance, the fear contracts to something proportionate, something you can work with.

From Scarcity Thinking to Agency Thinking

Looking at your financial reality clearly can set off a particular kind of thinking. When the numbers aren't where you want them to be, and for most people, at most points in their lives, they aren't, the mind moves quickly toward a scarcity frame: I'll never have enough. I'm bad at this. There's no point. This thinking is understandable, but it is also a trap, because scarcity thinking produces exactly two responses: avoidance or panic. Neither one moves the needle.

Agency thinking starts from the same facts, the same numbers, the same gap between where you are and where you want to be, and asks a different question: given what I have, what is my next right move? It doesn't require optimism about the situation. It requires only the willingness to locate the place where you have influence and put your attention there.

Scarcity: 'I'll never have enough.' → Avoidance or panic

Agency: 'What is my next right move?' → Action

The difference between these two frames is not a matter of personality or disposition. It is a decision you make, consciously, about where to direct your thinking. Scarcity asks what is wrong and who is to blame. Agency asks what is possible and what can be done now. You don't need to banish the scarcity thoughts; they will arise, because you're human and money is genuinely high-stakes. You need only to notice them and redirect: not 'I'll never have enough,' but 'What's one thing I can improve this month?'

This is not positive thinking. It is not a reframe that pretends the problem is smaller than it is. It is a deliberate choice to focus on the lever you can pull, rather than the gap you cannot close in a single step. That choice, repeated over time, is what financial self-leadership looks like in practice.

Taking Charge: The Financial Inventory

You cannot lead what you don't know. This is as true of your finances as it is of anything else, and it is the reason that the first act of financial self-leadership is not a plan or a goal, it is a clear-eyed look at the current reality.

1. Income: All sources of monthly income.
2. Fixed Expenses: Rent/mortgage, utilities, insurance, subscriptions, debt payments.

3. Variable Expenses: Food, transportation, entertainment, shopping.
4. Debt: Total balances across all accounts.
5. Savings & Assets: All savings and investment accounts.

For many women, this is the most uncomfortable step, more uncomfortable than making changes, more uncomfortable than difficult conversations, because it removes the ambiguity that avoidance depends on. Once you've done a complete financial inventory, you know. And knowing commits you to responding.

The purpose of this inventory is not to judge yourself. Your numbers are information, not a verdict on your worth or competence. What you find may be better than you feared, or it may be worse. It may be complicated in ways that require more attention than a single sitting. Whatever it is, it is the truth, and the truth is always more useful than a comfortable guess.

Do this exercise in a single sitting if possible, not because it needs to be comprehensive on the first pass, but because spreading it over multiple days makes it easier to stop before you've finished. Give yourself an hour, a quiet space, access to your accounts and statements, and the willingness to write down what you find. Fixed monthly income. Fixed monthly expenses: rent or mortgage, utilities, insurance, subscriptions, debt payments. Variable expenses: food, transportation, entertainment, shopping, anything that changes month to month. Debt totals, across all accounts. Savings and assets. The number left when you subtract your total monthly expenses from your total monthly income.

That last number tells you a great deal. If it's positive, you have choices about where to direct the surplus. If it's negative or smaller than you thought, you have specific information about where to focus. Either way, you are no longer guessing. You are working with reality, and reality is where all real progress begins.

Making Financial Decisions From Your Own Values

Once you know your numbers, the question becomes: what do you do with the choices you have? Financial self-leadership means making money decisions based on your own values and goals, not social pressure, not what your family expects, not what someone else thinks you should want.

This sounds obvious. In practice, it's far from it. Most of us have absorbed a complex web of messages about what money is for, what it signals, what it means to spend or save in particular ways. We buy things to signal belonging, to avoid conflict, to manage other people's impressions of us. We save or don't save based on patterns we inherited rather than priorities we've chosen. We make financial decisions, in other words, from everyone's values but our own.

Clarifying what you value, not in the abstract, but in the specific context of money, changes how decisions feel. When you know that security matters more to you than status, the choice to drive an older car while building your emergency fund doesn't feel like deprivation. When you know that experience matters more to you than accumulation, the decision to spend money on a trip rather than a possession isn't impulsive, it's intentional. Values don't make financial decisions easy, but they make them yours.

The practice is this: before a significant financial decision, get explicit about what you value in this context. Not what you're supposed to value, not what someone else would choose, what you actually care about. Then look at your options and ask which one honors those values most directly. The decision that emerges from that process is one you can own, and owning your decisions, even imperfect ones, is the foundation of financial self-leadership.

The Emergency Fund as Self-Leadership Tool

An emergency fund is, on one level, a financial tool: a buffer against the unexpected, a way to handle the car repair or the medical bill without going into debt or dismantling other financial plans. On another level, and this is the level that matters most for our purposes, it is an autonomy tool. It is the thing that makes it possible to choose.

Savings → Stability → Choice → Autonomy

Think about what changes when you have three to six months of expenses saved and accessible. You can leave a job that has become untenable without waiting until you have another one lined up. You can say no to the project that pays well but conflicts with your values. You can absorb a setback, a gap between jobs, an unexpected expense, a year when things don't go to plan, without it cascading into crisis. You can make decisions from a place of relative stability rather than desperation.

The rescue fantasy, at its core, is about the belief that your circumstances need to change before you can act freely. The emergency fund is one of the most direct ways to change your circumstances yourself. It doesn't require a windfall or a high income or a dramatic shift in your life situation. It requires consistent, intentional saving, even in small amounts, over time. The size of the first deposit is almost irrelevant. What matters is that it exists, that you added to it deliberately, and that it is yours.

Building an emergency fund is not the only component of financial autonomy, and it won't solve every problem. But for women who have operated with very little margin, financial or otherwise, it is often the single change that makes the most difference to how much freedom they experience in their day-to-day choices. Security is not a feeling you wait for; it is something you build.

When Financial Help Becomes Financial Control

Not all financial difficulty is self-imposed. Some women are in situations where someone else's involvement in their finances is not incidental but structural: a partner who manages all household money, parents who provide support that comes with strings attached, a family system where financial dependence is expected or even demanded. This is worth addressing directly, because the framework of individual self-leadership can be misleading when the obstacle isn't a personal pattern but an external constraint.

The distinction that matters is between help and control. Help looks like support that expands your options: money given without conditions, assistance that you can accept or decline, financial involvement that increases your capacity to make your own choices. Control looks like the opposite: money that comes with conditions attached, support that requires your compliance with someone else's preferences, financial arrangements that make you more dependent rather than less.

Control doesn't always announce itself. It can look like generosity on the surface, parents who pay rent, a partner who handles all the accounts, someone who says they're just trying to make your life easier. The test is not the dollar amount or the stated intention. The test is whether the arrangement leaves you more or less able to make your own decisions. If someone's financial involvement in your life is regularly being used, explicitly or implicitly, to influence what you do, where you live, what work you take, or what relationships you maintain, that is control, regardless of how it is framed.

Disentangling from financial control is rarely simple or quick. It often involves short-term sacrifice: a smaller apartment, a tighter budget, real discomfort in exchange for real freedom. It may also involve difficult conversations, changed relationships, and the loss of a kind of support that was genuine even when it was also constraining. None of that makes it not worth doing. The question is whether the cost of the arrangement—in autonomy, in self-direction, in the ability to build a life that is truly yours—is a cost you're willing to keep paying.

REAL STORY

Mara was twenty-eight and had never made a major decision without her parents' money in the equation. They paid her rent on an apartment they'd helped choose. They'd bought her car. They covered the gap between what she earned and what she spent without ever making a formal arrangement, just a transfer here, a dinner paid there. She'd told herself this was just practical. Her parents had money. They liked helping. Why would she refuse?

But then she started noticing the cost. When she brought her long-term boyfriend home after graduate school, her father disapproved and the relationship unraveled. When she wanted to move to a different city for a job opportunity, her parents said, 'Not while we're still supporting you.' The money was real. The affection was real. And the constraint was equally real.

Mara spent the better part of a year quietly making herself financially independent, and it was not comfortable. She moved to a cheaper apartment, sold the car, took public transit, ate simply, worked more than she would have chosen to. She was, by most external measures, worse off. And she was also, for the first time in her adult life, making decisions that belonged entirely to her.

A year later, she was stable; not wealthy, not without stress, but stable. The discomfort had been real. So was the relief. And her parents respected her for it.

Mara's story is a clear version of a dynamic that often looks much subtler. The financial control in your life may not be as direct or as explicit, it may be a soft expectation, an implicit understanding, a dependence you've chosen not to examine too closely because examining it would require changing it. The question is the same regardless of the form: is the support in your life expanding your choices or narrowing them? And are you willing to know the answer?

Small Financial Acts of Self-Leadership

Financial self-leadership does not require that you have everything sorted before you begin. It does not require a certain income level, a particular relationship status, or the complete elimination of debt. It requires only that you start practicing it in small, concrete, repeatable ways, starting now.

What this looks like in practice is a set of regular, intentional actions: checking your account balances instead of hoping they're fine. Reviewing your spending periodically so you know exactly where your money is going. Making at least one spending decision each week that is driven by your values rather than impulse or social pressure. Saving something, any amount, consistently. Opening the financial mail. Having the money conversation you've been postponing. Paying one thing on time and noticing that you did it.

These are not dramatic interventions. They are habits, and habits are what financial self-leadership is built from. Each small action reinforces the central message to yourself: I am the one who manages this. I am in charge of my financial life. That belief, repeated in practice often enough, changes your relationship to money more fundamentally than any single large decision.

The muscle of financial self-leadership is like any other muscle: it develops through use. The more consistently you make intentional financial decisions, even small ones, even imperfect ones, the more naturally you occupy the role of someone who directs her own financial life. And that role, once inhabited, changes everything else that follows from it.

ACTION STEPS

1. **Complete a Financial Inventory:** Do a real, sit-down-with-all-your-accounts inventory of where you really are. Income, expenses, debt, savings. All of it in writing, this week.
2. **Start (or Restart) an Emergency Fund:** Even if you can only put ten dollars in it right now. The amount is not the point; the act of creating the account, making the first transfer, and establishing the practice is.
3. **Practice One Financial Act of Self-Leadership Daily:** For the next two weeks, choose something small and specific: checking your balance, reviewing last week's spending, or making one purchasing decision based on your stated values rather than impulse. The goal is to build the habit of being the person who pays attention to her own financial life.

Moving Forward

Financial self-leadership is not a destination. It is a practice: the ongoing discipline of staying in the driver's seat of your financial life even when it's uncomfortable, even when the numbers aren't where you want them, even when it would be easier to hand the wheel to someone else. The work you've done in this chapter, looking clearly, thinking from agency rather than scarcity, building the habit of intentional financial decisions, is the same work the rest of this book has been pointing toward from the beginning. You are not waiting for external conditions to improve before you start directing your life. You are directing it now, with what you have, from where you are.

In the next chapter, we turn to the question of relationships, specifically, the ways capable women can find themselves organizing their choices, their ambitions, and their sense of self around what others need or expect. The rescue fantasy doesn't only operate through money. It operates through connection, and understanding how is the next part of the work.

CHAPTER 10

Your Support System

Designing Relationships That Strengthen Your Agency

— —

Self-leadership is not a solitary project. The idea that becoming more self-directed means becoming more self-contained, needing less from others, depending on no one, going it alone, is one of the more persistent myths around this kind of work, and it is worth dismantling early. The question is never whether to have support. It is what kind of support you choose, and what you allow that support to do.

The rescue fantasy shows up in relationships just as reliably as anywhere else. Sometimes it looks like waiting for the right person to appear and make decisions feel easier. Sometimes it looks like organizing your entire support structure around one or two people who, whether they mean to or not, end up doing the thinking for you. Sometimes it looks like tolerating relationships that quietly keep you smaller, where the unspoken contract is that you stay uncertain and they stay needed.

This chapter is about building a support system that works differently: one that increases your capacity rather than substituting for it, that holds you accountable rather than rescuing you from accountability, and that you choose deliberately rather than inherit by default. The distinction between support and rescue is subtle in some cases and stark in others, but it is always consequential, because the kind of help you accept shapes the kind of person you become.

The Difference Between Support and Rescue

Good support and rescue can look almost identical from the outside. Both involve someone showing up when things are hard. Both involve someone caring about the outcome. The difference is in what they leave behind.

Rescue → Immediate relief → Reduced autonomy over time

Support → Reflection + accountability → Increased autonomy over time

Rescue solves the immediate problem and leaves your capacity unchanged, or, over time, diminished. Someone makes the call you were dreading. Someone steps in and handles the situation you were avoiding. Someone takes the decision off your plate when you're uncertain. In the moment, this feels like relief. Across months and years, it quietly erodes your confidence in your own ability to handle things. You start to need the rescue more, not less. The person doing the rescuing—even if their intentions are entirely kind—becomes structurally necessary, and you become structurally dependent.

Support operates differently. It helps you think rather than think for you. It holds the thread of your own commitment back to you when you've lost it. It provides resources, information, or perspective, and then steps back, letting you make the call. It believes in your capacity to handle what you're facing and communicates that belief directly, without taking over. Good support increases your ability to function independently. The measure of it is not how much better you feel in the moment, but how much more capable you are over time.

This distinction matters enormously when you're examining the relationships in your life. Some of the people who love you most are rescuing you in ways that keep you stuck. They mean well. Their intentions are not the problem. The pattern is the problem, and the pattern can only change if you name it and make a different request.

Good support increases your capacity. Rescue decreases it. If someone's help consistently leaves you less able to act independently, it is not support, it is dependency, regardless of how it is framed.

Mapping Your Current Support System

Before you can build a better support system, you need to see clearly what you currently have, and what you don't. Most people have never done this inventory deliberately. Support tends to accumulate the way furniture does: you acquire it at different points in your life, it gets rearranged occasionally, and at some point you look around and realize the configuration is not quite right but you're not sure how it got that way.

A complete support system covers several distinct functions.

Emotional support: the people you can be honest with about what's happening, who listen without trying to immediately fix or redirect.

Practical help: the people who assist with tangible tasks when circumstances genuinely require it.

Accountability: the people who hold you to your own commitments without letting you off the hook, and without judgment when you fall short.

Expertise and mentorship: the people who have knowledge or experience in areas you're actively building, who can inform your decisions without making them for you.

Honest feedback: the people who will tell you what you need to hear, not just what you want to hear, and who have the relationship with you to make that useful rather than just uncomfortable.

And finally, celebration: the people who are genuinely glad when things go well for you, who mark your progress rather than minimizing it.

Most people have significant coverage in one or two of these areas and significant gaps in others. The most common gap is accountability, partly because it requires a particular kind of relationship where someone cares enough to stay engaged but not enough to just fix things for you, and partly because most of us have never explicitly asked for that from anyone.

The second most common gap is honest feedback. We tend to build support systems that affirm rather than challenge, which feels safer but ultimately serves us less well. A circle of people who always agree with you is not a support system. It is an echo chamber, and it will keep you exactly where you are.

The exercise of mapping your support system is valuable precisely because it moves you from an impressionistic sense of 'I have people I can count on' to a specific picture of who provides what, where the dependencies are, and where the gaps are. Once you have that picture, you can make deliberate decisions about how to strengthen it.

Identifying Support Gaps

Looking at the map of your current support honestly will likely reveal patterns you've been operating around without quite naming. The most significant gaps are usually not about the people who are absent, they are about the functions that are absent or distorted.

Over-reliance on one person for multiple types of support is one of the most common distortions. When your partner is also your primary accountability partner, your main source of honest feedback, and your emotional anchor, you've created a single point of failure in your support architecture, and you've also created a pressure in that relationship that it was probably not designed to hold. No single person can or should provide everything you need. Distributing the functions of a good support system across multiple relationships is not a sign of emotional unavailability. It is a sign of maturity.

Another common gap is the absence of people who are ahead of you. Mentors and models, people who have done the thing you're trying to do, or who are further along the path you're on, serve a function that peers, however supportive, cannot. They make the next stage feel real and achievable. They can see around the corners you haven't reached yet. They have information born of experience that no amount of encouragement can substitute for. If your support system contains only people at your level or below, you are missing this function entirely.

The most uncomfortable gap to look at is often this one: people who are technically providing 'support' but who are, in practice, keeping you smaller. The friend who always has a reason why your plan might not work. The family member who brings up every previous attempt that didn't pan out. The colleague who asks supportive-sounding questions that consistently redirect you toward caution and away from action. These are not bad people. But the impact of their involvement on your decision-making and confidence is worth examining. Support that repeatedly contracts your confidence or autonomy should be re-evaluated or restructured.

Building Support That Enables Leadership

Building a support system that genuinely enables your self-leadership is, above all, an active process. It requires you to know what you need, ask for it specifically, and be willing to redirect relationships that are currently configured in ways that don't serve you.

Knowing what you need sounds obvious but is often harder than it appears. Many of us default to receiving whatever support is offered rather than identifying what we genuinely need and seeking that out. The distinction matters because these are often different things. What's offered is usually comfort, agreement, and reassurance. What's needed is often clarity, challenge, and the experience of being held accountable to your own stated intentions. Getting clear on which of these you're looking for before you initiate a conversation will change how the conversation goes.

Asking specifically is the second piece. Vague requests for support produce vague responses that often default to rescue. 'I need help with this' invites someone to take it off your hands. 'I'm working on this thing, and what would be helpful is if you could check in with me on Friday about whether I've done the first step' is a completely different request; one that keeps you in the lead while drawing on someone else's presence and investment. The more precisely you can articulate what you need, the more likely you are to get it.

Choosing people who respect your autonomy is the third piece, and the most fundamental. Some people in your life will understand the difference between support and rescue intuitively and be glad to provide the former. Others will find it uncomfortable, because rescue satisfies something for them too, whether that's the feeling of being needed, the avoidance of tension, or a genuine belief that taking over is the most loving thing they can do. Both types of people can be in your life. Not all of them belong in your inner support circle.

REAL STORY

Lisa had known her closest friend since university, and for most of their friendship she'd been grateful for exactly the quality that she was beginning to see differently: her friend was a fixer. When Lisa had a problem, her friend had a solution. When Lisa was overwhelmed, her friend stepped in. It had felt, for years, like unconditional care.

Then Lisa started noticing, slowly, the other side of it. When she'd navigated something difficult on her own, her friend's response was more ambivalent than celebratory, a subtle steering back toward 'but you could have called me.' When Lisa didn't have a problem to bring, the dynamic between them became oddly flat.

The friendship had been built, without either of them realizing it, on Lisa needing help and her friend providing it. The conversation that followed was one of the more difficult ones Lisa had initiated. She told her friend what she'd noticed, not as an accusation, but as an honest account of a pattern she needed to change. She said: 'I don't need you to fix things for me anymore. What I need is for you to believe I can handle them, and to tell me that. Can you do that?' Her friend was quiet for a moment, then said yes. The friendship shifted. It got more equal. Lisa's confidence, in the months that followed, grew in direct proportion to how much less often she called looking for rescue.

What Lisa's story illustrates is that changing your support system sometimes means having difficult conversations with people you care about, not because they've done something wrong, but because the configuration has stopped serving you, and you need to name that directly. The people worth keeping in your inner circle will be able to hear it. The conversation itself is an act of self-leadership:

you are deciding what you need and asking for it clearly, rather than waiting for things to shift on their own.

The Role of Community

Individual relationships are not the only form support takes. Communities, groups of people navigating similar territory, sharing experiences, holding common commitments, provide something that one-to-one relationships often cannot: the experience of not being alone in a particular kind of challenge, at scale.

When you are the only person in your immediate circle who is trying to build something, change something, or step into a bigger version of yourself, that project can start to feel aberrant, like an exception to what people like you do. Being part of a community of people who are doing similar things normalizes the effort. It shows you what's possible in concrete rather than abstract terms. It provides models: women who are further along, who have faced the same obstacles and kept going, whose existence confirms that the thing you're attempting is real and achievable.

Community also provides accountability through shared commitment in a way that individual relationships don't quite replicate. When a group of people is all working toward something similar, showing up, doing the thing, reporting back, staying in the effort, becomes the baseline expectation rather than an exceptional achievement. The social dimension of shared commitment is a legitimate motivating force, and using it is not a sign of insufficient self-discipline. It is a recognition that humans are social creatures and that the right environment makes the work considerably easier.

The communities worth seeking out are the ones organized around what you are trying to build or become, not just around shared circumstances or shared identity. A group of women who are all stuck in the same way is company, but it is not necessarily support. A group of women who are all actively trying to move, who are practicing self-direction, building things, taking on challenges, offers something more useful. Seek out the latter.

When to Let Go of Support That Isn't Serving You

Not all relationships can be redirected, and not all of them should be maintained at the same level indefinitely. Some relationships in your life are genuinely incompatible with the version of yourself you are building, not because the people involved are bad or ill-intentioned, but because the relationship was formed around a version of you that is no longer accurate, and neither party knows how to navigate the gap.

The signs are usually recognizable, even when they're uncomfortable to acknowledge. You consistently feel less confident after interacting with this person than you did before. Your ideas feel smaller in their presence, your certainty less solid, your sense of what's possible more contracted. They may not be saying anything overtly negative, it may be in the questions they ask, the pauses before they respond to your news, the way they frame your ambitions as things that might not work out. The impact accumulates.

Sometimes this is about a relationship that was genuinely supportive at an earlier stage of your life and has not evolved. Some friendships and family relationships are organized around who you were when they began, and when you change significantly, the relationship can start to function as a pull back toward the earlier version rather than support for the current one. This is painful to recognize, and it doesn't mean the relationship has no value. It means the relationship needs to change, and that change begins with you naming what you're noticing and making a clear request.

Letting go, whether fully or partially, whether through distance or through explicit conversation, is not betrayal. It is a recognition that your support system is a living thing that needs to be tended deliberately. You are allowed to make choices about who has close access to your thinking, your decisions, and your sense of self. That is not selfishness. It is stewardship.

ACTION STEPS

1. **Map Your Current Support System:** Do a support system inventory on paper, mapping each function of support against the people who currently fill it. Identify genuine sources of accountability, truth-tellers, and mentors. Seeing the picture clearly is the prerequisite for building a better one.

2. **Make One Specific Support Request This Week:** Instead of a general 'I could use your help,' make a precise, structured ask: 'This is what I'm working on, this is the specific kind of support that would really help, this is what I'm not looking for.' Practice the language of asking for support that enables your leadership rather than substituting for it.

3. **Set One boundary Around a Relationship Configured as Rescue:** This may be a direct conversation or a quiet internal decision to stop bringing certain things to certain people. Make it a deliberate, conscious, and chosen decision rather than something that just happens.

Moving Forward

The people around you are not incidental to the work of self-leadership. They are part of the infrastructure of it. A support system that increases your capacity, holds you accountable, tells you the truth, and believes in what you're building is one of the most consequential assets you can develop, not because it will do the work for you, but because it will make it significantly easier to do the work yourself.

In the next chapter, we look at the arc of all the work this book has been building toward: what it looks like when you stop waiting and start moving, not as a one-time dramatic gesture, but as a sustained, daily practice of directing your own life with intention and clarity. The rescue fantasy ends not with a single decision but with a way of being. That is where we are headed.

CHAPTER 11

Creating Meaning Without External Milestones

Designing Meaning Through Values Rather Than Cultural Scripts

— —

There is a script most of us absorbed long before we had any say in the matter. It tells us what a meaningful life looks like: the relationship by a certain age, the house, the children, the title, the recognition. It tells us what counts as progress and what counts as falling behind. And it is so deeply embedded, so thoroughly reinforced by family and media and the questions people ask at holiday dinners, that many women spend years pursuing milestones that were never theirs to begin with, and feel obscurely empty when they arrive at them.

The rescue fantasy, in this context, operates through borrowed meaning. It is the belief that once the right external markers are in place, the relationship is official, the promotion secured, the house purchased, you will finally feel like your life has properly begun.

The problem is not the milestones themselves. Partnership, homeownership, career advancement, these things can be deeply meaningful. The problem is treating them as the source of meaning rather than the expression of it. When the milestone is doing the work of generating meaning that should be coming from inside, reaching it provides only temporary relief before the next one becomes necessary.

This chapter is about something more demanding and more durable: building meaning that is genuinely yours. Not borrowed from cultural scripts, not dependent on external validation, not contingent on achieving the next marker. Meaning that comes from living in sustained alignment with what you value, and from having the clarity to know what that is.

The Problem with Borrowed Milestones

The cultural script is not arbitrary. The milestones it prescribes, partnership, children, property, professional advancement, are things that carry genuine weight for many people. The issue is not that these things lack meaning. The issue is that when you pursue them because the script says you should, rather than because they align with what you have identified as mattering to you, you are building a life on a borrowed foundation.

You can hit every marker and still feel the persistent sense that something is missing, because the markers were never tracking what you needed them to track in the first place. The marriage happened, and the life you were waiting for didn't begin with it. The promotion arrived, and the satisfaction was real but brief. The house was purchased, and within months it was simply where you lived. The script promised that these things would mean something, and they do, but not the thing you needed them to mean. Not the feeling of being fully, recognizably yourself, living in ways that match your actual values.

This is one of the quieter forms of the rescue fantasy: the belief that the right external circumstance will finally produce the internal experience of a life well-lived. It is a fantasy because that causation runs in the wrong direction. External circumstances can support a meaningful life, but they cannot generate one. Meaning is produced from the inside out, from clarity about what matters to you, and from daily choices that honor that clarity.

You can also miss every cultural marker and build something genuinely rich. Women who have chosen not to partner, not to have children, not to pursue conventional career paths, who have instead organized their lives around what they most value, often describe a kind of aliveness and self-recognition that the checklist-completers are still searching for. The milestones are not the point. The values underneath them are the point. And those values are yours to identify, whether or not they map onto what the script prescribed.

Meaning comes from living according to your values, not from checking boxes on someone else's list. The milestone is not the point. What the milestone is meant to express—that is the point.

Identifying Your Actual Values

Values clarification is one of the most useful and least straightforward exercises in self-directed work. It is easy to produce a list of things that sound like they should matter to you. It is considerably harder to get honest about what truly does.

The values worth building around are not the ones that look good on paper or make you sound like a thoughtful person. They are the ones that, when you are living in alignment with them, produce a sense of being recognizably yourself and, when you violate them, produce the quiet friction of inauthenticity that is hard to name but impossible to ignore. Security. Freedom. Learning. Creative expression. Deep connection. Contribution to something larger. Excellence in a craft. Adventure. Integrity. These are examples, not a complete list, and they mean different things to different people, which is the whole point.

One reliable way to identify your actual values is to look at where you feel most alive and most like yourself, and ask what those experiences have in common. Not the activities themselves, the underlying qualities they share. A woman who comes alive in long conversations, in mentoring a junior colleague, in calling a friend who is struggling, her value might be connection, or contribution, or both. A woman who feels most herself when she is learning something new, building a skill, reading widely, her value might be growth, or mastery, or intellectual freedom. The pattern across experiences actually reveals what is operating.

A second approach is to look at where you feel most depleted, most resentful, most like you are performing rather than living.

Resentment, in particular, is reliable information about value violation. When you are consistently doing things that violate your values, spending time in ways that feel hollow, making choices that contradict what you care about, the body keeps score before the mind catches up. Sustained depletion is often a signal that you are living against your values, whether or not you have named them explicitly.

The goal of this inquiry is not to produce a final, permanent list. Values clarify and evolve over time, and what matters most to you at thirty-five may look somewhat different from what mattered at twenty-five or will matter at fifty. The goal is to get specific enough about what currently matters most that you can use it as an actual guide, a reference point for decisions, a standard against which to measure how you are spending your time.

Designing Personal Milestones

Once you have some clarity about your actual values, you can do something the borrowed script never offered you: design milestones that genuinely mean something to you. Not milestones that someone else defined as markers of success, but milestones that mark progress toward the life you are really building.

What makes a personal milestone different from a cultural one is its relationship to your specific values. A cultural milestone is legible to everyone; it signals something within a shared framework of what a successful life looks like. A personal milestone may not be legible to anyone but you, and that is entirely the point. It marks something that matters by your own measure, not by consensus.

These milestones can be large or small. They can be achievement-oriented, finishing the project, having the conversation, making the move, or they can be process-oriented, marking sustained commitment to a practice rather than arrival at a destination. A woman who values creative expression might mark the milestone of completing a first draft, not because she expects to publish it but because completing it means she has acted on something she cared about rather than waiting for the right conditions to begin. A woman who values contribution might mark the milestone of a year of consistent volunteering, not because anyone is counting, but because she is.

The act of designing these milestones is itself significant. It requires you to be specific about what you want your life to contain and what you want to be able to say you did with your time. It is a declaration, even a quiet one, that your life will be measured by your own standards rather than borrowed ones. And it gives you something concrete to move toward, which is more useful than the vague intention to 'live according to your values,' however genuine that intention is.

Micro-Meaning in Daily Life

Milestones, whether cultural or personal, mark significant moments on a long arc. But meaning is not only, or even primarily, found in those moments. It is found in the ordinary texture of daily life, in the small choices that either align with or diverge from what you care about, repeated hundreds of times across weeks and months and years.

Values → Daily choices → Alignment evidence → Identity reinforcement

This is where the practical work of values-based living happens. Not in the grand gesture or the major decision, but in how you spend a Tuesday afternoon, in whether you make the phone call you've been putting off, in what you say yes to and what you decline, in whether the way you spent today reflects anything you genuinely care about. These small alignments, or small betrayals, accumulate into the felt experience of a life. The person who finishes each day with a sense of having lived according to what matters is not someone who had an unusually meaningful day. She is someone who has built the habit of daily alignment.

Building that habit does not require grand reorganization. It requires developing the practice of asking, regularly, whether what you are doing now is connected to what you have identified as meaningful. Not in a way that produces constant self-interrogation or anxiety, but in the way that an athlete occasionally checks her form, not because something is wrong, but because small corrections made consistently prevent significant drift over time.

The payoff is cumulative. Each small act of living in alignment with your values generates evidence, felt, embodied evidence, that you are someone who does this. That identity, built through small consistent choices, is far more stable than meaning that depends on reaching the next milestone. It is also far harder to take from you. The milestone can be delayed, denied, or rendered moot by changing circumstances. The practice of daily alignment is entirely within your control.

REAL STORY

Janet was forty-two when she stopped measuring her life against the cultural checklist long enough to really look at what it contained. No partner, no children, no mortgage, no corner office. By the metrics she'd been using without quite choosing them, she was behind. The question that had been nagging at her for years, whether she was doing life right, had produced a persistent low-grade dissatisfaction that she'd attributed to the missing markers.

What changed was a conversation with a coach who asked her: 'What do you actually want your days to feel like?' Not your five-year plan. Not what you're working toward. What do you want the ordinary texture of your life to be? Janet sat with the question for a week before she could answer it clearly. She came back with three things: she wanted to be constantly learning something. She wanted to feel like her presence in other people's lives made a concrete difference. And she wanted the freedom to move, to reorganize her life around new interests without having to dismantle a fixed structure to do it.

When she looked honestly at her life against those three values, she found something unexpected: it was already full of them. She was learning constantly, courses, books, conversations with people who knew things she didn't. She was contributing in ways that were visible and appreciated, mentoring, volunteering, showing up for people. Her work gave her the flexibility she valued. The life she had was not behind. It was, by her actual measures, abundant. The dissatisfaction had been borrowed from a script that was never tracking what she cared about. Once she stopped using that script as her measure, it dissolved almost entirely.

Janet's story is not an argument against wanting partnership, or homeownership, or professional advancement, any of which might genuinely matter to you. It is an argument for knowing the difference between what you truly want and what you have been told you should want. That distinction, honestly investigated, changes how you measure your own life. And it changes what you spend your energy pursuing.

When Others Don't Understand Your Path

Living by your own values rather than the cultural script will generate questions. Some of them will be genuinely curious. Many will be a version of the same underlying assumption: that the standard milestones are the correct measure of a life, and that departing from them requires explanation.

Be clear about this: you do not owe anyone a justification for how you are living. The questions people ask—when are you getting married, don't you want children, when will you buy a house, what's your five-year plan—are often not requests for information. They are expressions of a framework that treats the conventional path as the default and everything else as deviation. You cannot satisfy that framework by explaining your values, because the framework is not looking for an explanation. It is looking for confirmation that you're on track.

The most useful thing you can develop is not a set of scripted responses to these questions, but a settled internal relationship with your own choices. When you are genuinely clear about why you are living the way you are, when the decisions you've made are connected to values you have examined and chosen, other people's confusion or concern becomes considerably less destabilizing.

You do not need them to understand. You need to understand, and that clarity is available to you regardless of whether anyone else shares it.

That said, some responses are more useful than others. 'I'm focused on what matters to me right now' is not a conversation-stopper, it is an honest statement. 'I've thought about it carefully and I'm happy with where things are' invites no further debate. The tone that works is not defensive and not apologetic. It is the tone of someone who has made a decision she is at peace with, and who is not particularly interested in relitigating it. That tone is only accessible when the internal clarity is genuinely there, which is why the values work comes first.

Building Your Own Traditions

One of the things the cultural script provides, beyond milestones, is ritual, ways of marking what matters, celebrating transitions, and acknowledging progress. When you step off the conventional path, you step away from these ready-made rituals as well. The birthday where everyone asks about your relationship status. The wedding that marks arrival at adulthood by cultural consensus. The promotion announcement that signals to the room that you have succeeded. These rituals have meaning embedded in them, even when the underlying assumptions are ones you have consciously rejected.

The answer is not to do without ritual. It is to build your own. A tradition does not need to be witnessed or sanctioned by others to carry weight. The annual solo trip you take every year to mark your birthday. The practice of reviewing what you have built or learned at the close of each year, without reference to anyone else's metrics. The celebration dinner you host for yourself when you finish something that mattered to you. The ritual, however simple, of acknowledging that you showed up for something you cared about.

These self-designed traditions serve a function beyond celebration. They train your attention toward what is truly meaningful in your life, rather than what is conventionally legible. Over time, they build a private record, a felt history of your own choices and their alignment with your values. That record is an anchor. When the cultural script reasserts itself loudly, as it will, having your own tradition of marking what matters gives you something to stand on.

The traditions worth building are ones that feel genuinely yours, not performances for anyone else, not compensations for what you have opted out of, but authentic acknowledgments of what your life really contains. Design them with the same care you bring to your milestones: rooted in your values, specific enough to be real, and yours to keep regardless of anyone else's understanding of their significance.

ACTION STEPS

1. **Values Clarification:** Spend time with questions like: Where do you feel most alive and like yourself? Where do you feel most depleted? What experiences across your life would you want more of, and what do they have in common? What do your most regretted choices have in common? The answers are reliable indicators of your actual values.

2. **Design Personal Milestones:** Design three to five personal milestones explicitly rooted in your identified values, not cultural scripts. Make them specific enough to know when you've reached them, and meaningful to you regardless of external understanding.
3. **Practice Daily Alignment:** Begin the practice of daily alignment by asking, at the close of each day or week, whether your time reflected anything you care about. A single, honest question regularly asked is enough to build evidence that you live according to what matters.

Moving Forward

Creating meaning on your own terms is not a one-time act of redefinition. It is an ongoing practice of staying honest about what matters to you, measuring your life by the right metrics, and making choices, large and small, that reflect your actual values rather than borrowed ones. The rescue fantasy, at its core, is about outsourcing meaning: waiting for the right external circumstances to produce the internal experience of a life well-lived. What this chapter has been building toward is the opposite: the recognition that meaning is made, not found, and that you are already equipped to make it.

In the final chapter, we bring together everything this book has covered, and look at what it means to move forward from here. Not as someone who has completed a process, but as someone who has built a practice. The rescue fantasy ends not with a single breakthrough but with a sustained, daily commitment to leading your own life. That is where we are headed.

CHAPTER 12

The Practice of Self-Celebration

Acknowledging Your Progress as Self-Leadership

— —

There is a particular kind of woman who is very good at noticing everything she has not yet done, and almost constitutionally unable to register what she has. She finishes a project and immediately sees its flaws. She reaches a goal and shifts her attention to the next one before the first has been properly acknowledged. She deflects compliments with practiced ease, attributes her successes to luck or circumstance or the contributions of others, and maintains a running internal commentary that is far more rigorous about failure than it is about progress.

This is not modesty. Modesty is a considered choice about how to present oneself. What this describes is something more automatic: a structural inability to let evidence of your own competence land. And it matters, not just as a quality-of-life issue, but as a practical obstacle to self-leadership, because if you cannot take in the evidence that you are capable, that evidence cannot do its work. You remain, internally, someone who is not yet sure she can handle things, regardless of how much external proof accumulates.

Self-celebration is the practice of closing that gap. Not performance, not ego, not the public announcement of your achievements. The private, intentional act of letting your wins register, of saying to yourself, clearly and without deflection, that you did something difficult and you are aware of it. This chapter is about building that practice, starting from wherever you currently are.

Why Self-Celebration Matters

Self-celebration is a practical tool before it is anything else. When you acknowledge your wins, however small, you are building something concrete: a body of evidence about your own competence that you can draw on when doubt arises. And doubt will arise. The inner critic does not go quiet because you have decided to be kinder to yourself. It goes quiet because you have accumulated enough counter-evidence, registered often enough and deliberately enough, that it can no longer dominate the conversation.

This is especially important for work that is not publicly visible. Much of the most significant progress in self-leadership, the decision made with less anxiety than before, the boundary held, the difficult conversation finally had, the thing done without waiting for perfect conditions, happens invisibly. There is no external recognition because there is no external observer. If you do not register these wins yourself, they will not be registered at all. The forward movement you are making will not count in your own accounting, and you will continue to feel stuck even as you are, in fact, moving.

Self-celebration also reinforces the behavior it celebrates. When you acknowledge that you did a hard thing, you are telling yourself, in a language the body understands before the mind catches up, that doing hard things is something you do. That identity becomes self-fulfilling. The woman who regularly notices her own courage becomes, incrementally, more courageous. Not because she has convinced herself she is fearless, but because she has built a practiced relationship with the experience of doing difficult things and registering that she did them.

And self-celebration breaks the dependency on external validation that lies at the heart of the rescue fantasy. If your sense of your own progress depends on whether others notice and name it, you have outsourced a fundamental part of your self-assessment to people who may be preoccupied, oblivious, or simply not positioned to see what you are doing. Taking that function back, becoming your own reliable witness, is one of the most genuinely autonomy-building things you can do.

Self-celebration is especially important when you are doing work that isn't publicly visible or traditionally valued. If you wait for external recognition, you may wait indefinitely. The practice of noticing your own progress is not optional; it is the whole infrastructure.

What Counts as a Win

The first obstacle most people encounter with self-celebration is definitional: what actually counts? The habit of dismissal is usually attached to a very narrow definition of what is worth acknowledging, promotions, completions, external recognition, measurable outcomes. By that standard, the days, weeks, and months between major achievements contain almost nothing worth noting. Which is both false and corrosive. A more useful framework recognizes at least four distinct categories of wins, each of which is genuinely worth acknowledging:

1. **Outcome Win:** The promotion, the finished project, the award, the milestone reached. These are real and worth celebrating, but relatively rare.
2. **Process Win:** You showed up when you didn't feel like it, you kept going when it was tedious, you maintained the habit through a difficult week, you did the next right thing without requiring yourself to have all the subsequent steps worked out first. These build momentum and are often invisible by conventional standards.
3. **Character Win:** You honored a value when it cost you something to do so, you held a boundary that was uncomfortable to hold, you made a choice that reflected who you are trying to become rather than who you've defaulted to being. These are about integrity rather than achievement.
4. **Courage Win:** You did the thing scared. You made the ask, spoke the truth, took the risk, attempted the thing you had been circling for months. The act of doing it in the presence of fear is the win, regardless of the outcome. Expanding what you count as worth acknowledging is not about lowering standards. It is about accurately tracking the full range of your own progress, which includes a great deal more than the narrow band conventional achievement metrics capture.

The Weekly Wins Practice

The most practical form of regular self-celebration is a simple, consistent weekly practice: at the end of each week, identify at least three things that went well or that you are genuinely glad you did. At least one of these should come from outside the traditional outcome category, a process win, a character win, a courage win. Write them down. This last part is not optional.

Writing matters because it externalizes the acknowledgment in a way that makes it harder to immediately dismiss. The internal acknowledgment, the brief moment of 'that went well', is too easy to override. It happens, and then the internal critic comes back with context: 'but it's not really that significant,' 'anyone would have done that,' 'you still haven't done the harder thing.' The written record is more durable. It stands as evidence even when your mood, your confidence, or your inner critic's current volume would tell you otherwise.

Over time, the written record also serves a second function: it becomes a resource. When you hit a stretch where nothing feels like it is going right, and those stretches will come, you have an actual archive of evidence that contradicts that feeling. The wins were real. They happened. They are there in your own handwriting, not as motivational content but as a factual account of what you have been doing and who you have been becoming.

Consistency matters more than comprehensiveness in this practice. Three honest wins a week, acknowledged in writing, maintained over months, will do more for your self-assessment than an occasional burst of enthusiastic journaling followed by a long gap. The regularity trains your attention to look for what is going well in the moment, which gradually rebalances a perceptual system that has been weighted toward noticing what is not.

When Celebrating Feels Uncomfortable

Many women find self-celebration genuinely uncomfortable, and the discomfort is worth examining rather than simply pushing through. It usually has a source. Somewhere in the formation of who you learned to be, there was a message—direct or ambient, stated or modeled, that acknowledging your own accomplishments is the same thing as claiming you are better than other people. That celebrating yourself is unseemly. That modesty requires minimization.

These messages are worth naming clearly because they are doing active damage. The equation between self-acknowledgment and arrogance is a false one, and it is disproportionately applied to women. Men who acknowledge their accomplishments are described as confident. Women who acknowledge theirs are more often described as boastful, self-promoting, or 'a lot.' The result is that many capable women have internalized a prohibition against letting their own wins count, which means they are operating without the fuel that self-acknowledgment provides.

Self-acknowledgment is an honest accounting of what you have done. 'I did something difficult and I am proud of it' is not a comparative statement. It does not require anyone else to be diminished. It is a private recognition of your own effort and capability.

If the discomfort is strong, start small. The goal is not immediate fluency in self-celebration. It is graduated exposure to the experience of letting a win register without immediately deflecting it. Five seconds of genuine acknowledgment before the dismissal moves in. Ten seconds. Saying 'thank you' to a compliment instead of 'oh, it was nothing.' Writing one true thing down at the end of a day. Each small practice builds the tolerance for acknowledgment that makes the larger practice possible.

REAL STORY

Rachel had been taught, with great consistency as a child, that talking about your own achievements was showing off. Drawing attention to yourself was a kind of social transgression, a signal that you thought too highly of yourself. When she finished her master's degree after three years of part-time study while working full-time, she told almost no one. It felt like bragging. When she was promoted at work, she spent the announcement conversation redirecting the conversation away from herself.

The discomfort of being celebrated was acute. The shift came when a coach asked her a question she hadn't considered: 'What does it cost you to not acknowledge this?' Not in terms of other people's perceptions, in terms of her own internal experience. What she noticed, when she sat with the question, was a pervasive flatness. She was producing results constantly and feeling almost nothing from them, because she never let herself fully receive what she had done. The acknowledgment had been systematically blocked, and the block was preventing her from building the felt sense of her own capability that might have made the next challenge feel more manageable.

> She started with very small steps. Writing three things she was glad she had done at the end of each week. Saying 'thank you, I worked hard on it' instead of 'it was nothing, really' when someone commented positively on her work. Letting herself feel the satisfaction of a completed project for sixty seconds before moving to the next task. Over several months, something shifted, not in her outer circumstances, but in how she experienced herself. She stopped feeling like someone waiting to be found out, and started feeling like someone with a track record. That track record had always been there. She had simply refused to acknowledge it.

What Rachel's story makes clear is that self-celebration is not about adding something artificial to your experience. It is about removing the block that has been preventing something real from reaching you. The wins are already happening. The practice is learning to let them count.

Celebration Rituals

Practices become habits when they are attached to structure. A wins journal kept in the same place, opened at the same time each week, becomes something different from a good intention, it becomes a routine, which means it happens with far less activation energy than anything that requires deciding to do it from scratch each time.

The rituals worth building operate at different time scales, and each serves a slightly different function. A daily acknowledgment, something as simple as naming one thing at the end of the day that you are glad you did, written or spoken aloud, keeps your attention oriented toward progress rather than deficit. It is not elaborate, and it should not be. The point is consistency, not ceremony.

A weekly practice is where the more substantive reflection happens: three wins minimum, drawn from across the categories, written down. This is also a useful moment to notice what kind of wins are showing up. If your list is consistently all outcome wins, you are probably undercounting your process and character progress. If your list feels thin, that is information too, either you are being too selective about what counts, or it has been a week that genuinely requires you to look more carefully.

Monthly and major-milestone celebrations can be more deliberate: a dinner, an experience, a specific acknowledgment that matches the scale of what was accomplished. These are markers, and markers matter because they interrupt the tendency to move immediately from one thing to the next without registering the transition. The brain benefits from being told, clearly and repeatedly, that something has been completed, that it mattered, and that the person who completed it is capable and worth attending to.

Design your rituals to fit your actual life and your genuine preferences. The best celebration ritual is one you will do consistently over time. It does not need to be impressive. It needs to be yours.

Sharing Wins Strategically

Self-celebration does not have to be private. Sharing your wins, selectively, with the right people, is both legitimate and useful. It reinforces the win through articulation, it allows others who care about you to genuinely participate in your progress, and it models something that is in short supply: women speaking directly about what they have accomplished without apology or deflection.

The word 'selectively' carries most of the weight in that sentence. Not everyone in your life is equipped to celebrate with you. Some people will minimize—not always from malice, but because your progress makes them aware of their own stagnation, or because they have the same prohibition against self-acknowledgment that you are trying to dismantle, and hearing you celebrate feels like a social transgression. Some people will immediately redirect to themselves: 'That's great, actually, something similar happened to me...' Some people will respond with a version of 'but what about...' that immediately pulls the conversation toward what still needs to be done.

These are not the people to bring your wins to. Bringing wins to people who cannot hold them well does two things: it diminishes the win through the interaction, and it trains you to associate celebration with social risk, which makes you less likely to celebrate at all. The solution is not to stop sharing; it is to be deliberate about who you share with.

The people worth sharing wins with are the ones who can genuinely participate in your good news, who celebrate without competing, who hold the moment with you rather than rushing past it, who are glad for you in a way that is uncomplicated by their own agenda. You likely know who these people are. The practice is to bring your wins to them specifically, rather than to whoever happens to be around, and to notice the difference in how the sharing lands.

ACTION STEPS

1. **Start a 'weekly wins' practice this week.** Not when you have a better system in place, not when things settle down, but this week. Choose a day and time (Friday afternoon, Sunday evening, whenever works for your schedule), and commit to writing down at least three wins before the week closes. Make at least one of them a process, character, or courage win rather than an outcome win. Keep the record somewhere you will see it again.
2. **Design one celebration ritual** that you will use. Not the most elaborate version, not the aspirational version, but the version you will stick to. A two-minute end-of-day acknowledgment practice. A weekly wins journal entry. A monthly dinner you take yourself to when you've hit a significant marker. Choose one, make it specific, and start this week.
3. **Practice self-acknowledgment** in the small, daily interactions where dismissal has become automatic. When you complete something, let yourself feel it for a moment before moving to the next thing. When someone offers a compliment, practice receiving it rather than deflecting it. Say 'thank you, I worked hard on that' instead of minimizing. Each instance of this practice is its own small win, and it is worth acknowledging as such.

Moving Forward

The practice of self-celebration is, at its core, the practice of being your own reliable witness. Not your harshest critic, not your most indulgent cheerleader, your honest, attentive, consistent witness. The one who notices what you do, registers that it happened, and keeps an accurate account of who you are becoming.

This is the final chapter before the conclusion of this book, and it lands here deliberately. Everything else covered in these pages—understanding the rescue fantasy, building self-leadership, taking action without waiting for perfect conditions, making decisions from your own values, building support that enables rather than rescues—requires fuel. Self-celebration is that fuel. It is what makes the practice sustainable over the long arc, not just in the energized early weeks. You cannot keep moving forward if you never stop to register that you have moved at all.

Before we move on to the next chapter, take a moment with this: you have done something in picking up this book and working through it. That is not nothing. Let it count.

CHAPTER 13

Leading Through Uncertainty

Developing the Capacity to Act Without Guarantees

— —

Uncertainty is not a temporary condition you endure until things become clearer. It is the permanent state of any life being actively directed, and one of the most reliable markers of whether someone has accepted that reality or is still working against it. The woman who is waiting for certainty before she acts, waiting until she knows how it will turn out, until the risks are smaller, until she has enough information to be confident, is not being careful. She is refusing to engage with the actual conditions of a self-directed life.

This is one of the places the rescue fantasy is most seductive. If you are waiting for someone or something to arrive and make the path clearer, a mentor who gives you the definitive answer, a sign that confirms your direction, a set of circumstances that removes the ambiguity, you are, in effect, waiting for someone else to absorb the uncertainty for you. What you are waiting for is not information. It is rescue.

That rescue will not come. Uncertainty does not resolve itself in advance of action. It resolves, or more precisely, transforms, afterward, through action, through information gathered in the doing rather than the deliberating, through the experience of having moved and discovered what moving produces. The uncomfortable truth at the heart of this chapter is that the only way out of uncertainty is through it: not around it, not with someone rescuing you from it, not by waiting long enough for it to diminish. Through it. This chapter is about how.

Why We Freeze in Uncertainty

The pull toward stillness in the face of uncertainty is not weakness. It is biology. The brain's threat-detection system responds to unpredictability in much the same way it responds to physical danger, by prioritizing protection over progress, caution over action, the known over the unknown. When you cannot predict the outcome of a decision, the part of your nervous system that is designed to keep you safe activates, and it generates a familiar set of responses: the desire for more information, the search for guarantees, the postponement of commitment, the impulse to find someone who can tell you what to do.

These responses feel like prudence. They feel like responsible preparation. But they have a characteristic that careful preparation does not: they are never satisfied. The information gathered never feels sufficient. The guarantees sought are never offered. The postponement extends indefinitely. What looks like diligence is, in practice, the elaboration of a waiting pattern, and the waiting is not making the decision easier. It is making it harder, because with each delay the stakes feel higher, the decision feels more loaded, and the threshold of certainty required before action rises rather than falls.

The other thing these responses do is protect a particular story: that you would act if only you knew more, if only the path were clearer, if only the risk were smaller. This story is almost always false. The information available is almost always enough to make a workable decision. The risk is almost always manageable. What is not yet present is the willingness to act without a guarantee, and no amount of additional information will supply that willingness. It is a capacity that has to be developed, not a threshold that will eventually be crossed through sufficient preparation.

Understanding why the freeze happens does not eliminate it. But it changes the relationship to it. When you recognize the pull toward more information or more certainty as a predictable response to unpredictability, not as a signal that more preparation is genuinely needed, you can make a deliberate choice about whether to follow it. You can acknowledge the discomfort without letting it make the decision for you.

The goal is not to eliminate uncertainty. It is to build your capacity to act within it, to move forward with the information you have rather than waiting for the certainty that will never fully arrive. Certainty doesn't come before action. It comes after.

Building Uncertainty Tolerance

Tolerance for uncertainty is not a fixed trait. It is a capacity, and like any capacity, it develops through use. The woman who seems to move through ambiguous decisions with relative ease is not simply built differently. She has, over time and through accumulated experience, developed evidence that she can handle not knowing how things will turn out, because she has not known how things would turn out many times before, moved anyway, and survived the experience. Often more than survived it.

The mechanism here is straightforward: every time you make a decision in the presence of uncertainty and the world does not end, your tolerance for the next uncertain decision increases slightly. Not because the uncertainty diminishes, the next decision will be just as uncertain, but because your working model of your own capacity becomes more accurate. You are building a track record that the part of your brain looking for historical evidence of survivability can consult.

This means the path to handling larger uncertainty runs through smaller uncertainty first. Not as a rigid progression, but as a deliberate practice of noticing that you already make uncertain decisions regularly and mostly handle them. The restaurant you chose without knowing whether it would be good. The route you took without knowing whether it was the fastest. The conversation you initiated without knowing how it would land. These are all decisions made in the presence of not-knowing. You make them constantly, and they almost never produce the kind of catastrophe that the threat-detection system suggests is possible.

The practice is to begin extending this awareness to progressively higher-stakes decisions: to notice where you are already tolerating uncertainty effectively, and to carry that evidence forward into contexts where the stakes feel higher. The question to ask is not 'how do I make this decision with certainty' but rather: 'I have handled not-knowing before. What do I already know about how I do that?' The answer to that question is more useful than any additional information gathered in the service of eliminating uncertainty that cannot be eliminated.

The Clear Criteria Framework

Most of us make decisions one of two ways. The first is to search for the perfect option, the one that, if you had all the information and all the time in the world, you would choose above everything else. The second is to decide in advance what a good, workable choice looks like, find something that meets those criteria, and commit to it.

The first approach sounds more rigorous. In practice, it is usually the engine of paralysis. Searching for the perfect option means comparing every available option, which means gathering more information, which is both time-consuming and ultimately impossible, because you cannot fully evaluate a choice without actually making it. The result is an extended holding pattern: accumulating information that adds less and less value, postponing commitment in the name of being thorough, and frequently arriving at a decision later and more exhausted, having made no better choice than you would have made three months earlier.

The second approach works differently. It starts not with 'what is the best option?' but with 'what does a good-enough choice require?'

You set your criteria in advance; not everything you would ideally want, but the things that must be present for a decision to work. Then the process becomes straightforward: does this option meet those criteria? If yes, it's a candidate. If more than one candidate exists, pick one and move.

The hardest part of this approach is the commitment to stop searching once a workable option is found. Because the impulse toward perfection doesn't disappear the moment you find something good, it generates a question: 'but what if there's something better?' There almost certainly is something better, somewhere. There always is. The real question is whether finding it is worth the cost of continuing to look, weighed against the value of acting now with something that works. For most decisions, delay costs more than the difference between good and perfect.

This is not the same as settling. Settling implies resignation, a sense that you deserve more than you're accepting. This is something different: you have identified what really matters, found something that delivers it, and made a clear-eyed choice to act rather than keep searching. That is not resignation. That is clarity about what you are actually trying to achieve.

Scenario Planning for Major Uncertainty

For decisions where the stakes are high and the uncertainty is genuine, scenario planning is a practical tool for working through what you are facing. Not to achieve certainty, but to get an honest look at the realistic range of outcomes, including the one you are most afraid of.

The exercise has three parts:

1. **Best Case:** Clarifies what you are hoping for, which is information about your values and motivation.
2. **Worst Case:** The critical question is not what happens if everything goes wrong, but whether you can handle it if it does. Most worst-case scenarios, when examined honestly, turn out to be survivable.
3. **Most Likely Case:** The realistic middle ground between what you hope for and what you fear, and in most cases, it represents a workable outcome. This is where the decision should be anchored.

The best-case scenario matters because it clarifies what you are actually hoping for, which is information about your values and motivation. But it is not where the useful work happens. The worst-case scenario is where most of the productive thinking occurs, because the critical question is not what happens if everything goes wrong, but whether you can handle it if it does. This question deserves a direct answer, not an avoidance. Most worst-case scenarios, when examined honestly rather than catastrophized about vaguely, turn out to be survivable. Difficult, costly, requiring adjustment, but survivable. And knowing that changes the risk calculus significantly.

The most likely scenario is where the decision should be anchored. It is the realistic middle ground between what you hope for and what you fear, and in most cases, it represents a workable outcome, not ideal, not catastrophic, but manageable. When you make your decision from the most likely scenario rather than from either extreme, you are making it from the actual territory rather than from the best or worst version of the map.

The final question scenario planning should produce is not 'which scenario will occur?', you cannot know that. It is: having looked honestly at the realistic range of outcomes, including the worst, does proceeding still make sense? And if the worst occurs, do I believe I can handle it? If the answer to both is yes, you have the information you need to move.

REAL STORY

Andrea had been offered a position with an international organization, work she had trained for, in a city she had always wanted to live in, with people she respected. The offer represented almost everything she had said she wanted. And she couldn't make herself accept it. The information-gathering phase lasted three months. She researched the city exhaustively. She spoke to everyone she could find who had lived there. She asked for extensions on the decision deadline twice. She made lists of pros and cons so detailed they became useless. What she was really doing, though she didn't name it this way at the time, was searching for a guarantee she could not have: that she would be happy there, that she would make friends, that she could handle being far from her family, that the role would be what she imagined it would be.

The conversation that broke the logjam came from a mentor who had known her for years. She said: 'You're not going to get certainty on this. That's not what's on offer. What's on offer is a choice between two kinds of uncertainty, the uncertainty of going, and the uncertainty of not going and spending years wondering what would have happened. You get to pick which uncertainty you'd rather live with.

> That's the whole decision.' Andrea realized she hadn't seen that staying was also uncertain, also a risk, just a less visible one. She took the role. She chose to experience what no amount of pre-departure research could have taught her, and proved that she was capable of handling what she could not predict. That knowledge was worth more than the certainty she had been searching for.

Andrea's mentor gave her a reframe that is worth keeping: staying is not the safe option. Inaction under uncertainty is not the absence of risk; it is a different risk with its own costs, including the ongoing cost of not knowing what would have happened. When you understand that all options carry uncertainty, the question changes from 'how do I avoid the uncertain choice?' to 'which uncertainty am I willing to live with?' That is a question you can answer.

When Uncertainty Generates Anxiety: Reading the Signal

Uncertainty and anxiety frequently travel together, and it is worth developing the ability to distinguish between them, not to dismiss the anxiety, but to avoid letting it do work it is not equipped to do. Anxiety in the face of uncertainty is almost always a signal about the presence of uncertainty, not about the specific quality of the decision you are facing. It does not reliably tell you whether to proceed. It tells you that you are in uncertain territory, which you already knew.

What can be more useful is learning to distinguish between anxiety-driven concern and a genuine, specific reservation. Anxiety-driven concern has certain recognizable qualities: it is general rather than specific, generating a vague but pervasive sense of unease rather than a clear objection. It tends toward catastrophizing: the feared outcome is typically extreme, and the path from current circumstances to that outcome is not clearly mapped. It feels like noise: persistent, cycling, difficult to quiet with information because it is not asking for information.

A genuine reservation looks different. It is specific: not 'this might go wrong' but 'I don't yet have clarity on this particular aspect, and without it I can't evaluate the decision accurately.' It points somewhere actionable: there is a question that could be investigated, a conversation that could be had, a piece of information that would genuinely change the assessment. And it tends to be quieter than anxiety, less insistent, more like a clear note than static.

The practical implication of this distinction is that genuine reservations deserve investigation and anxiety does not deserve to make the decision. When you notice something that feels like a concern, the first question is: can I name what specifically worries me? If the answer is yes and the concern is specific and addressable, address it. If the answer is no, if the worry is general, ambient, and resists specification, it is likely anxiety about uncertainty itself, and the most useful response is to acknowledge it, note that it is present, and move forward anyway.

This is not about ignoring signals your body is sending. It is about reading them accurately. The signal that uncertainty sends is not 'do not proceed.' It is 'you are in uncertain territory.' That is information about conditions, not a verdict on the decision. You are capable of being in uncertain territory. You have been there before.

What You Already Know About Handling Uncertainty

One of the most underused resources in navigating uncertainty is your own history with it. Every woman reading this book has made uncertain decisions before—decisions where she did not know how things would turn out, where the outcome was not guaranteed, where she moved anyway. She has a track record with uncertainty. She is usually not consulting it.

The reason the track record goes unconsulted is partly structural: the brain's threat-detection system is much better at cataloguing what went wrong than at building an accessible record of what went right and what was survived. The decision that turned out badly is more vivid and more available than the decision made in uncertainty that turned out fine, or the decision made in uncertainty that turned out badly but was survived anyway. Both are evidence of capacity. Neither tends to be held as such.

Building an active evidence base means deliberately surfacing this history. What are the uncertain decisions you have made? What happened? What did you learn about your own capacity from the experience, not just about whether the outcome was good, but about whether you handled it? The answer, in almost every case, will be: yes, you handled it. You adjusted. You found your footing. You kept going. This is not motivational content. It is an accurate account of a track record that already exists and that is directly relevant to the uncertain decision you are facing now.

The questions worth asking yourself before a difficult uncertain decision are: What is the most uncertain decision I have made in the past year, and what happened? What did I learn about myself from navigating uncertainty I didn't know how to resolve? What resources, internal and external, did I draw on? The answers orient you toward your own demonstrated competence rather than toward the hypothetical threat that uncertainty generates. They are grounding in the most literal sense: they put you in contact with what is really true about you, rather than what fear suggests might be true.

ACTION STEPS

1. **Create an evidence audit:** identify three decisions you have made in the past two years where the outcome was genuinely uncertain at the time you made them. For each one, note what you did, what happened, and, most importantly, what you discovered about your capacity to handle not knowing. Do this in writing, with enough specificity that it functions as actual evidence rather than vague reassurance. This record is your working history with uncertainty. Consult it.
2. **Apply the satisficing framework** to a decision you are currently stuck on. Satisficing means choosing the first option that meets your minimum criteria rather than searching for the perfect one. The word is a blend of "satisfying" and "sufficing," coined by economist Herbert Simon; it's based on the principle that, in real decisions, the cost of finding the perfect option usually outweighs the benefit.

Before doing anything else, get explicit about your minimum criteria: not everything you would ideally want, but what must be true for a choice to be workable. Then survey your options against that list rather than against an implicit standard of perfection. If an option meets your criteria, it is a candidate. If multiple candidates exist, choose one and commit to it. Stop searching for the option that would make you certain, because that option does not exist.

3. **Build a personal toolkit** for the moments when uncertainty generates strong enough discomfort to make forward movement feel impossible. This toolkit is not a list of coping mechanisms; it is a set of deliberate practices that interrupt the freeze and return you to agency. It might include specific questions to ask yourself: What do I actually know, as distinct from what I am imagining? What is the next smallest step I can take? What would I tell a close friend who faced this decision? It might include people you can think out loud with, not people who will tell you what to do, but people who will help you think more clearly. It might include reference to your evidence base. Whatever it contains, having it built and available before the moment of strong uncertainty means you do not have to construct it from scratch at the moment you most need it.

Moving Forward

The capacity to act under uncertainty is not separable from the capacity to lead yourself. Every significant decision in a self-directed life is made without a guarantee. Every step toward something you want is a step into not-knowing. The woman who has developed genuine tolerance for that condition, who can move forward despite the discomfort, who knows from experience that she can handle what she does not know in advance, is not a different kind of person from you. She is you, having practiced.

In the final chapter of this book, we bring together the full arc of everything covered here, the rescue fantasy, the patterns that sustain it, the practices that dismantle it, and look at what it means to carry this work forward. Not as a set of techniques to deploy when things get hard, but as a way of being in your own life: present, capable, moving, and no longer waiting for someone or something to make the way clear. That is where we are headed.

CHAPTER 14

Your Ongoing Practice

Sustaining Self-Leadership Beyond the Book

— —

You have arrived at the final chapter of this book. That is worth acknowledging, not as a formality, but as a fact. You picked this up, you worked through it, and you are here. That is not a small thing. The women who most need what this book contains are also the women most practiced at talking themselves out of finishing things, at finding reasons why the timing is not quite right, at telling themselves they will come back to it later when they have more capacity. You did not do that. You kept going. That is already evidence of the thing this book has been trying to build.

Now comes the question to answer honestly: what happens next? Not in the motivational sense, not the implied promise that everything is different now that the old patterns are gone, that you will walk out of these pages permanently transformed. But in the practical sense. Self-leadership is not a destination you reach by finishing a book. It is a practice, ongoing, imperfect, requiring maintenance. And the transition from working through a book to living the practice it describes is where most good intentions stop being intentions and become something actual. Or don't.

This chapter is about making sure yours do. It covers the rhythms of ongoing practice, what to do when you slip back, because you will, and how to carry what you have built here into the life that continues after you close these pages. And what becomes possible when you stop organizing your life around a rescue that was never going to come.

Self-Leadership as Lifelong Practice

There is a particular temptation at the end of a book like this, and it is worth naming. It is the temptation to treat the completion of it as an arrival, to feel the satisfaction of finishing and mistake that satisfaction for transformation. The reading is done, the ideas have landed, and something has shifted. Something has. But what has shifted is understanding, and understanding alone does not change a life. Practice does.

Practice → Evidence → Adjustment → Continued practice

Let's use the analogy of fitness. No one finishes a week-long fitness program and considers themselves permanently fit. The weeks built something real: capacity, habit, a different relationship with the activity, but the capacity requires use to be maintained. Stop using it and it diminishes. Continue using it and it grows. The same is entirely true of self-leadership. The practices in this book are not techniques to deploy once when you encounter the relevant problem. They are ways of operating that require repetition to become genuinely yours.

What this means practically is that the goal after finishing this book is not to remember everything in it. It is to identify the two or three practices that matter most to you right now—the ones that address your specific version of the waiting pattern, the areas where your self-leadership is weakest and the development of which would most change your experience of your own life—and to build those into your regular rhythm. Not all of them at once. Not a comprehensive overhaul. A sustainable start, maintained consistently over time.

Progress in self-leadership is not linear. There are periods of genuine momentum where decisions feel cleaner, where the old pull toward waiting is quieter, where you operate from a surer sense of your own authority, and there are periods where the old patterns reassert themselves with a force that can feel like going back to zero. You are not going back to zero. You are encountering one of the recurring tests that a practice of self-leadership always presents: can you notice the slip, understand what produced it, and return to yourself without the return requiring a crisis?

The answer, built through the practices in this book and the years of practice that follow it, is yes. Not immediately, not effortlessly, and not without sometimes needing support. But yes.

The Monthly Check-In

Sustained practice requires periodic honest assessment, not to grade yourself, but to stay oriented. Without regular check-ins, the drift back toward old patterns can happen slowly enough that you don't notice it until you are well off course. A monthly review interrupts that drift before it becomes a problem.

The monthly check-in is a simple practice: once a month, in a quiet space with no agenda other than honest reflection, you look at the past thirty days through the lens of self-leadership. Not productivity or achievement in the conventional sense, but specifically: where did you act from your own authority? Where did you make decisions that were genuinely yours, based on your values, without waiting for permission or external validation? Where did you hold a boundary that needed holding? Where did the old pattern of waiting or deferring show up, and what produced it?

This last question, 'where did I wait when I could have moved?', is the most important one, and the most uncomfortable. The instinct is to pass over it quickly, to note it and move on. The practice is to stay with it long enough to understand it. Not to judge yourself for the pattern, but to get curious about its conditions: what was happening when the waiting showed up? What did you tell yourself that made waiting feel justified? What would it have looked like to make a different choice? Understanding the conditions of the pattern is how you interrupt it earlier next time.

The monthly check-in should also include deliberate acknowledgment of what went well, not as compensation for the harder questions, but because the evidence of your own progress is a resource you need to actively build. The wins of a month disappear quickly from memory if you do not record them. Written down and reviewed, they become something you can stand on when doubt arises: proof, in your own words, of what you have been doing and who you have been becoming.

The Annual Review

Once a year, on your birthday, at the new year, at whatever marker carries weight for you, the monthly practice expands into something larger: a full accounting of the year through the lens of self-leadership. Not a performance review, not a comparison to an external standard, but a genuine, unhurried reckoning with how you directed your own life across twelve months.

The most useful questions for an annual review are ones that can only be answered with a year's worth of evidence behind them. How have you grown in your capacity to make decisions from your own authority? In what areas of your life are you most free, most genuinely operating from your own values and choices rather than from external expectation or the residue of old patterns? In what areas does the waiting pattern still have the strongest hold, and what does that tell you about where the work continues?

The annual review is also the right moment to reassess your values and milestones. The values clarification you did earlier in this book was accurate at the time you did it. A year of lived experience will have refined it. Things that felt central may have receded; things you undervalued may have proven essential. The milestones you set may have been reached, abandoned as wrong for you, or revised in light of what you learned. This is not inconsistency. It is the natural update that comes from a year of living according to your choices and discovering what they produce.

End the annual review with a forward look that is specific rather than aspirational. Not 'I want to be more confident' but 'I am going to have the career conversation I have been postponing, and I am going to have it before the end of the first quarter.' Not 'I want to stop seeking external validation' but 'When I notice I am waiting for someone else's assessment before I act, I am going to name it, make my own assessment, and move.' Specificity is what converts intention into direction.

When You Slip Back Into Waiting

You will slip. This is not a possibility to prepare for; it is a certainty to accept. The patterns addressed in this book are not bad habits you developed last year. They are ways of operating that were built over a long period of time, reinforced by genuine experience, and woven into the way you have understood yourself and your place in the world. They do not evaporate because you have understood them clearly and decided to do otherwise. They recede, meaningfully, measurably, in ways you will notice, and they return, usually when conditions are right for them: stress, loss, uncertainty, the presence of someone who activates the old relational dynamic, a moment when your confidence in your own judgment has taken a hit.

The slip is not failure. It is information. It tells you something about the conditions under which the pattern still has purchase, which is useful because those conditions are the ones that most need your attention going forward. A woman who has done genuine work on self-leadership and then finds herself waiting for permission in a particular relationship or a particular domain of her life is not back at the beginning. She is encountering a specific edge of the pattern that still has work left in it.

The most important thing you can do when you notice you have slipped is to return to yourself without making the slip into a referendum on whether the work is real. The notice-and-return is the practice. It is not the evidence that the practice has failed. Every time you notice that the old pattern has activated and make a deliberate choice to move differently, you are reinforcing the capacity you have been building. The gap between slip and return may be years at the beginning of the work and hours later on. That narrowing is the whole measure of progress.

When you notice you've slipped, the sequence is simple: notice it without judgment—'I've been waiting for permission again'—get curious about what produced it, reconnect with your own evidence of capability, and take one small autonomous action today. Not a dramatic gesture of self-reclamation. One decision, made from your own authority is enough to interrupt the pattern and begin the return.

Slipping back into old patterns does not erase your progress. Every time you notice the pattern and choose differently, you are practicing the very skill this work is about. The notice-and-return is the practice, not the evidence that the practice has failed.

Carrying the Work Forward

The practices in this book are not equally useful to everyone, and they are not equally useful to you at every stage. Different chapters will be the ones you return to most, and that will shift as your life does. When you are facing a major uncertain decision, Chapter 13 is the one to revisit. When you find yourself seeking external validation before you trust your own assessment, Chapter 5. When a boundary has collapsed and you need to rebuild it, Chapter 6. When the old waiting pattern has reasserted itself and you need grounding in your own capability, Chapter 2 and the evidence base you have been building since.

Keep this book somewhere accessible, not as a trophy for having finished it, but as a working resource. The most useful books in a person's life are rarely the ones read once and placed on the shelf. They are the ones consulted, argued with, returned to when circumstances make them relevant again.

Beyond the book, the practices that will most sustain your self-leadership in the long run are the simplest ones: the weekly wins record that keeps your progress visible to you, the monthly check-in that keeps you honest about where the work continues, the support system that holds you accountable without rescuing you, and the ongoing practice of making decisions from your own values rather than from external expectation. These are not complicated. They are consistent. And consistency, maintained over time, is what changes a life.

Before you close this book, there is something that needs to be said directly. Not as a pep talk, you have had enough of those, but as an honest account of what is genuinely true about you.

You are not someone who lacks capability. You have never been that. The problem was never that you were not good enough, not ready enough, not capable enough to direct your own life. The problem was a story, quietly, persistently told, that your real life would begin later. After the right circumstances arrived. After someone confirmed you were ready. After the rescue came. That story kept you organized around a future that required nothing of you in the present, and it kept you from fully inhabiting the life that was already yours to lead.

Here is what is true instead. You have been making things work your whole life, often in conditions far less favorable than the ones you have been waiting for. You have handled situations you were not prepared for, navigated uncertainty without a map, made decisions with imperfect information and lived with the results. You have built things, maintained things, showed up for things when it cost you something to do so. The evidence of your capability is not hypothetical. It is historical. It is already there, in the record of what you have actually done.

The rescue fantasy was always solving the wrong problem. It was not a lack of competence that kept you stuck. It was a lack of permission, specifically, the permission you were waiting for someone else to grant. The central, quiet revelation of this book is that no one is coming to grant it. Not because you are undeserving, but because it was always yours to give. It has been yours all along.

What changes when you stop waiting is not your circumstances, at least not at first. What changes is your relationship to your own life, from spectator to participant, from someone waiting to be chosen to someone who chooses, from someone organizing her actions around what others will think or permit to someone who acts from the inside out. That shift is not dramatic. It does not announce itself. It shows up in small decisions, made with a little less hesitation than before. In boundaries held a little longer. In goals pursued a little more directly. In the accumulating sense, built through consistent small choices over time, that you are the one steering.

That sense is what this book has been building toward. Not confidence as a feeling, feelings come and go and cannot be reliably manufactured, but confidence as a demonstrated capacity, built through action, confirmed through experience, held as evidence that can be consulted when doubt arises. The confidence of someone who has done things and knows she has done them.

You will not do this perfectly. No one does. There will be months when the old patterns dominate and the practices fall away and the waiting reasserts itself with a completeness that makes the work you have done feel fragile. It is not fragile. The work you have done is in you, and you cannot unlearn what you have genuinely understood. You can only temporarily act as though you have forgotten it, and then remember, and return.

The returning is the whole practice. The returning, over and over, without shame and without drama, to the person you have become: someone who directs her own life with clarity and intention, who does not wait for circumstances to improve before she engages fully, who does not need external permission to trust her own judgment, who knows what she values and makes choices that reflect it, who acknowledges her own progress and builds on it rather than dismissing it.

That person is not someone you are trying to become. She is someone you already are, on the days you let yourself be. The work of this book, and of all the practice that follows it, is simply to increase the number of those days. To make the gap between who you are on your best days and who you are the rest of the time narrower and narrower, until the distance between them is small enough that you can no longer use it as a reason to wait.

You have already started. You started when you picked this book up. You continued every time you kept reading when the material was uncomfortable, every time you recognized yourself in a pattern you had not named before, every time you decided that understanding it was worth more than the comfort of not looking. That is not nothing. That is, in fact, the beginning of everything.

Your life does not begin when the rescue arrives. It has been happening all along. The question is only whether you will lead it.

You will. You already are.

About the Author

SM Dyer is a life coach with decades of global experience working with high-performing leaders. Many of her clients arrived carrying patterns they had never quite named: self-doubt, imposter syndrome, the quiet habit of waiting for validation or better conditions before fully stepping forward.

Her coaching focuses on interrupting inherited patterns that limit capable people, not through motivation or quick fixes, but through the kind of honest, practical work that produces lasting change.